HOW TO PLAY CONSISTENT GOLF

TOM KITE

AND LARRY DENNIS

Foreword by Bob Toski

GOLF DIGEST

POCKET BOOKS

New York London Toronto Sydney Tokyo Singapore

Published by:

NYT SPECIAL SERVICES, INC.
An Affiliate of the New York Times Company
5520 Park Avenue, Box 395
Trumbull, CT 06611-0395

and

POCKET BOOKS, a division of Simon & Schuster Inc.
1230 Avenue of the Americas, New York, NY 10020

Book Design by Dorothy Geiser

Photography by Steve Szurlej
Additional photographs by Larry Petrillo, Pete Lacker
and Pete Marovich

Illustrations by Nancy Miller

ISBN: 0-671-51098-3

Library of Congress Cataloging-in-Publication Number: 90-61658

First Golf Digest/Tennis, Inc. and Pocket Books
trade paperback printing November 1994

10 9 8 7 6 5 4 3 2 1

Printed in the U.S.A.

DEDICATION

To Mom and Dad, who encouraged me to play.
To Harvey Penick, who taught me how.
To Christy, who has made it all worthwhile.

TABLE OF CONTENTS

FOREWORD

Tom Kite is the best student I've ever had. I've never had a student so perceptive, so quick to pick out a fault in his swing and so much of a perfectionist.

I met Tom in 1973, early in his first full year on Tour. Frankly, I wasn't impressed with his golf swing, although I never told him that. Harvey Penick, one of the greatest teachers ever, had taught him how to play, which is the most important factor in making a good score. But I felt that Tom would have trouble putting together four good rounds of golf with the technique he was using at the time. He wasn't a good driver of the ball, he wasn't a good fairway wood player or long iron player. I knew his short game would sustain him, but I didn't know what he could do on a tough golf course that required good technique to control the ball for the entire tournament.

After I began working with Tom and realized what his attitude was and how realistic he was in his self-appraisal, I knew that in time he would succeed. There were television commentators and others who said he couldn't make it, that his swing wasn't good enough, that he couldn't do this or that. I never knocked his golf game. I knew he would make it. I just didn't know to what degree. I thought he could win two or three hundred thousand dollars a year out there and make a decent living. But, to be honest, I never thought he would become the leading money-winner of all time.

Too many players get intrigued by golf and become fascinated with making a number but are not willing to improve their technique so they can make that number. They sit around the grillroom and talk about it a lot, but they don't make the commitment to do it. They don't make a realistic appraisal of what it takes to improve. When they come to a teacher like me, I tell them what they have to do and ask them whether they want to do it or just talk about it. Most of them just want to talk about it. I've taught a lot of students who wait for things to happen. Tom Kite went out and *made* it happen.

Tom always has been inquisitive. He's a searcher. He asked me a lot of questions . . . and he understood the answers. And his determination, his tenacity in learning how to play golf better, is amazing. No one can realize how hard he has worked. He has gone from just an average Tour player to a super player. To take the golf swing he had when he first came to me and do what he has done is incredible.

Tom is a quiet man who goes about his work. You never see him sit down and moan about his game, talk about what he missed and what he made, where he blew it. He doesn't get down on himself. Tom is a doer and a thinker, and that to me is what has made him great. He has perseverance, he has pride, he has patience, and he knows how to practice. Through all his efforts to improve, he never lost his talent for scoring. Only a very few players have the knack of making a number while they're changing their swings. They never lose that feeling for being able to get the ball in the hole. Tom is one of those. He wanted to make his technique better, but he never lost sight of what is important, which is playing the game. Technique will carry you only so far. He is gifted with

After I realized what his attitude was, I knew in time he would succeed.

His determination, his tenacity in learning how to play golf, is amazing.

a wonderful sense of feel, as are all great players, and he used it to good advantage.

As soon as I saw that, I didn't have any qualms about changing his swing. Tom would call me to talk about his game, and I'd tell him to just go out and play golf the best he could, make the best number he could and learn from the experience. Then come back and we'd work on the swing again.

He now is one of the best ball-strikers out there, and as his technique improved, his scoring became more consistent, which has made him the most consistent player on Tour.

Now Tom has written a book that tells you how he achieved that consistency. It will tell you how you can do the same thing—how you can strike the ball better and, most important, how you can learn to *play* golf better and have more fun doing it. It may not make you a Tom Kite, because few have ever played the game as well, but it will make you a better player at your own level.

The thing that has impressed me more than anything else about Tom Kite is that he has always been a gentleman and a sportsman. He is recognized for that on Tour and throughout the world of golf, and that may be his most important quality. It's a quality to emulate whenever and wherever the game is played.

I have to add one more thing. I've always felt that behind every great player was an understanding wife, and I know of no one more understanding than Christy Kite. During all the hours I worked with Tom, Christy sat there and patiently listened and watched and tried to help him become better. She understood his ability and his desire to improve.

Back in my early days on Tour, I admired Ben Hogan's wife, Valerie, and Byron Nelson's wife, Louise. Since then, no wife had impressed me as much until I met Christy.

Tom might have become a great player without her support, but Christy certainly made it easier.

Bob Toski, Dean of Instruction
Golf Digest Schools

INTRODUCTION

"Would you
want me to try
less hard?"

This time it was January, a cold and drizzly day in Austin, Texas, when I called Tom Kite at home. Tom wasn't there, said Christy Kite, and somehow I knew what she was going to say next: "He's out practicing."

It didn't surprise me, because Tom Kite has been practicing ever since I've known him, which is ever since he arrived on the PGA Tour.

I was walking through a restaurant in Greensboro, North Carolina, in 1973 when Bob Toski hailed me over to his table. "I want you to meet Tom Kite," said Toski. "He's going to be a helluva player."

Little did we know.

Tom and I became friends, and I became an unabashed Kite fan. There was something in him that struck a chord. He was going to succeed no matter what, if only by working harder than everybody else. Many of us, maybe most of us, feel that way, but few do as much about it as Tom Kite has.

Sometimes he got in his own way, although he would be reluctant to admit it. I once accused him of trying too hard.

"The little engine that could" had become a great player.

"Would you have me try less hard?" he snapped. He had a point.

I don't know how many gnawing doubts, in the dark of the night, Kite has suffered. Probably many, but he's never made them public. The positive is all that ever shows.

Once, during one of his many lengthy streaks of making tournament cuts, a writer asked him when he planned to miss his next cut. Kite said, "Never."

"You mean you're never going to miss another cut?" the incredulous writer asked.

"No," Tom replied. "I'm never going to plan to miss one."

Kite sneaks up on you. During the 1970s, he was a solid player, even while remaking a swing that was not exactly Tour-caliber when he came out. He made a lot of money, finished consistently high, even won a couple of tournaments. He chugged along, and that became his reputation.

In 1981 he suddenly had the most consistent year anybody short of Byron Nelson has ever had. He finished in the top ten in 21 out of 26 tournaments. He was eighth or better in 17 of his last 18 starts. He won the money title. He won the Vardon Trophy with the fifth lowest scoring average ever. The nation's golf writers named him Player of the Year. But he won only one tournament, and nobody paid a lot of attention.

Still, that began an inexorable march. The victories came more often, and he was always there on the leaderboard. It took a while to figure out what was going on here. More wins in the decade than all but two players. A stalwart on six straight Ryder Cup teams. Two scoring titles. Player of the year a couple of times. A single-season money record. The leading money-winner of all time. "The little engine that could" had become one of the game's great players.

No, to this point he has not won a major, since The Players Championship does not yet count. He wants to. We all want him to. I suspect he will. But majors happen. Far lesser players than Tom Kite have won them. Few better players have. If he wins one or more, it will not, in my eyes, make him greater. If he doesn't, it will not make him less.

His quest for knowledge remains as frenetic as ever. He had and has his favorite gurus, but he still asks and listens to anybody he thinks might have information he can use—he used to ask me to watch his swing, which I guess only illustrates how indiscrimminate he was in his search. But he always has been able to sort it out. So he has been able to improve every year. And he has become perhaps the most consistent player in modern history, or maybe in all of history.

This book came about when some of us realized that Tom Kite may know more about the golf swing than anybody on Tour. When we finally got around to the writing, however, it turned out that *swing* was not the operative word. *Playing* was. *Scoring* was.

He always could play and score, and he has gotten better at it as the years have gone by. He also is having more fun at it, and he passes all this along to you.

You will learn a lot about Tom Kite in this book. You also will learn to make your fundamentals better and your practice more enjoyable and productive, which in turn will let you have a lot more fun playing a lot better golf.

Larry Dennis
Huntington, Connecticut
September, 1990

CHAPTER 1/ LEARNING TO PLAY GOLF

Scoring is the only thing that matters.

This book is about playing golf. Better golf. Consistently better golf. It's not about the swing, it's not about technique, it's not about working at golf or any of the other things that are being taught by a number of teachers today. It's about playing the game, how I have learned and am still learning and how you can, too.

There are a lot of golfers and their instructors who feel that improving their golf swings will automatically improve their games. They may, but they also may not. There is a pretty good chance that in the short run you could even score worse by improving your swing. And it's conceivable that, even in the long run, a swing change may not help.

This is not to say that we all can't improve our games by improving our golf swings. The pros on Tour make swing changes. I've made them all my life, probably every year. But I've been careful in the changes I've made and in the help I received in trying to make those changes. I don't change my golf swing just for the sake of change. I've always kept in mind that the only reason I was making swing changes was to *improve my ability to score.* When you get right down to it, *scoring is the only thing that matters.* "Pretty" is not where it's at. Scoring lower is what we all are trying to do. Depending on your handicap level, the repetitiveness of your swing and the amount of time you have to devote to the game, there are a lot of things you can do to improve your ability to play and to score that don't have anything at all to do with mechanics.

Anytime you make a change in your swing you can move in one of two directions—you can get better or worse. If you are a beginner or a poor player with an undeveloped swing, there is a long list of changes that could help and only a short list of changes that might hurt. The better you are, the greater your chances that a swing change may hurt you, and the list of those changes that could help becomes shorter. You need to make a commitment to all aspects of your game, a commitment to playing better golf rather than just improving your swing.

For example, a player who makes a swing change and begins to hit better shots could be taken out of his element, and he might not know how to handle it. Let's take a person who consistently hits only two or three greens a round but is an excellent chipper. He ends up with a lot of putts in the three-to-10-foot range, and he makes a lot of them. All of a sudden he improves his shotmaking ability and now hits eight or nine greens a round. But now he has a lot of longer putts. Since he cannot make as many putts from 20 to 40 feet as he did from closer in, he could become frustrated with his putting. He also may not be as good a putter from 30 feet as he is a chipper from 60 feet. He thinks he should be saving four or five strokes a round but he may not even save a full stroke. That could actually turn a positive into a negative. Now he is a better shotmaker but he may not have helped his score, and he's discouraged.

I've always tried to make my swing as good as possible, and I've made tremendous improvements in my swing over the years. But most of those improvements have resulted in

There is a lot of room in golf for individual differences.

an ability to score better because I've also focused on *playing golf.* I've always been aware that no matter how much I improved my swing and my shotmaking ability, that did not guarantee lower scores. I still had to pay attention to detail, to concentration, to doing the things that let me get the ball into the hole in fewer strokes.

Swing improvement and playing golf can go hand in hand, of course. Improving your swing is an admirable goal, and I'm all for anyone who wants to do it. All other things being equal, it's the best way to get your game to a higher level, as I'll discuss later. But you have to be aware that there is no reward for this in itself. You are never going to win a nassau bet with anyone just because you've improved your swing. You will only win that nassau because you shoot a lower score. To do that you have to play golf.

I'll guarantee that you can take the swing you have right now and improve your handicap by simply paying attention to the other factors involved in playing golf—your short game, your strategic approach, your emotional control. You can consistently play better by improving in these areas without touching your mechanics. If you want to advance to another level, as most of us do, then improve your swing. But don't forget that the main objective is still to play golf and make the best score possible.

I strongly believe that there is a lot of room in golf for individual differences. I really admire those players who do not have textbook form and still get the job done. There is no one best way to hit a golf ball. In fact, there are hundreds of ways that work. I see it on Tour every day. These are the best players in the world, and it's hard to find two who swing alike.

In this book, I'll give you the preshot fundamentals and the mechanics that I feel are basic to a good swing, those that are used by most of the Tour players. I'll also give you some ways to play golf better and more consistently, and I urge you to take advantage of these.

The way to play the best and most consistent golf you can

is to establish the swing mechanics that you can repeat as often as possible and translate them into a feel that works on the course. Then trust that feel when you have to pull off a shot. The ideal scenario is to have a perfect golf swing and to trust it totally. I don't know anybody who has accomplished both those goals. I know I haven't, and I doubt that you have, either. We all just try to get as close as possible. So how do we do that?

Maybe the best way is to learn the way we did when we were kids. Psychologists tell us we will learn 90 percent of what we will learn in life by the time we are 6 years old. And we learn all this basically by trial and error. We learn how to crawl, how to walk, how to drink out of a cup, how to talk, how to write . . . all of it by trying, incorporating what works and discarding what doesn't. It's called child's play. Children learn by playing. That's also not a bad way to learn golf. That's the way a 6-year-old would learn golf. It's the way I learned it. And even if you are a couple of days older than 6, the trial-and-error approach can work. Just go out and play. Learn what works for you and what doesn't.

Sure, you need some guidelines, which I'll give you. But fit those guidelines to your physical and mental makeup. Then practice to refine and improve. But practice effectively. A lot of people don't like to practice, so they don't do it, or they don't know how to practice, so it doesn't do them any good.

We read and hear a lot about *working* on our game on the practice tee, or the practice bunker, or the practice green, then going to the course and *playing* golf. I'm going to suggest a better way. I'm going to show you how to learn to play better golf by telling you how to *play practice* instead of working at practice. I'll suggest a bunch of games that will improve your ability to practice efficiently and have a good time doing it. The games will develop your technique and the skills required to play various shots, giving you a lot of diversification in your swing, especially in the short game. Then you'll have the confidence to play those shots on the course, where they count.

I'll also give you some guidelines for better using your mind, which is where you can make the most progress in this game.

I was about 6 when I started tagging along with my dad, Tom Sr., when he went out to practice. He was a good player—still is, in fact—and I picked up the game pretty quickly. I enjoyed it and I was decent at it, so it was easy to enjoy. I loved golf so much that I really never had a desire to play any other sport. I still love it, but don't ask me to explain why. I suppose you like chocolate ice cream because it tastes good. Well, golf feels good.

At the time we were living in Dallas. They had an excellent junior program under Joe Dreisbach, the pro at Riverlake Country Club, where my folks were members, and we could play and practice there all day during the summer. It was fun, and I was shooting in the 70s by the time I was 10 or 11. I had seen some professional tournaments in Dallas, and along about then I knew I was going to be on the PGA Tour someday. I suppose every kid who plays halfway decently dreams of that, but I *knew* it.

My education as a golfer didn't really kick into high gear, however, until we moved to Austin and joined the Austin Country Club, where Harvey Penick was the pro and the golf coach at the University of Texas with a reputation as a fine teacher. I remember the first lesson I took from him. I was 13 and scared to death. As we were going out to the practice tee, he talked with me about what I'd been doing and the scores I'd been shooting. Then he said, "We have a good junior high program, and I think our number one goal right now should be to make the junior high golf team. After that maybe we can make the high school team, and after that we can make the college team. I think those ought to be our goals right now."

That kind of shocked me. I knew I was going to be on the Tour, and I never had any thoughts about not making the junior high or high school or college teams. Those were just stepping-stones on the way to getting where I wanted to go.

As it turned out, that first lesson from Mr. Penick gave me the philosophy on which I've based my life and career. He was telling me to take things as they come and not get ahead of myself. Take care of business right now, do the best you can at this particular moment, and if you do that often enough you'll be good. If every day you learn something and every day you improve a little bit, even if it's a minuscule amount, you'll be moving in the right direction and sooner or later you'll get there.

I keep hearing the expression, "It's not how fast you get there but how long you last." I agree with that 100 percent. You've got to keep moving in the right direction, and everything I've tried to do has been to get me where I am now. Everything I'm doing right now is to try to get to a point that's better and will be for quite a while.

So I got a good foundation from Mr. Penick that very first day. It's a lesson everyone should learn. Most good things, especially golf, take time and patience to develop. Take it one step at a time and realize that every small improvement gets you closer to your goal.

I guess I gave myself every chance to improve. We were allowed to hit our own balls on the club's driving range, which was very wide. I could hit balls down the right side of the range and go pick them up and not get in anybody's way. I'd just go out and practice all the time. Dad used to go to work early, and in the summer months he'd drop me off at the club on his way. So I'd get there at 7 o'clock and hit balls for two hours before the rest of the kids showed up. Then we just packed our bags on our shoulders and went out to play. A lot of times we would play 18, then grab something to eat. A bunch of the guys would jump in the swimming pool for an hour. I'd go hit some more balls or putt. Then we would play another 18. Then it would be time for Dad to get off work, and maybe the two of us would play nine more. So on many days I'd play 36 or 45 holes as well as hit a lot of balls. But it was not work. It was fun. I could not have spent that much

> Take things as they come and don't get ahead of yourself.

time had it been work. I was doing just what I wanted to do.

I was really small when I was 13. I probably didn't weigh 100 pounds. But I had a good, solid golf swing. Then I started growing. I got heavier and the swing began to change a little bit. I developed a big "reverse C" on the follow-through. That was the "in" thing then, because that's what Jack Nicklaus was doing. I also developed a short, flat back-swing (which Nicklaus was not doing). Later on in my career I changed that, but there were some very good things about my early swing. I hit the ball fairly low but I could hit it like a rifle shot. I hated the windy days in Texas because I couldn't stack my practice shots one on top of the other. I was almost that accurate. And I wasn't bad for distance, especially if I could run the ball. I wasn't good at flying it, but in Texas that wasn't that big a deal. And I was still just trying to make the junior high team, you know.

Under Mr. Penick's guidance I really started to improve and became a good player. I think that's because he let me do some of those things in my swing that a lot of teachers wouldn't let a student do. I was a little wristier in my putting than I should have been, because on the Bermuda grass greens I grew up on you need to pop the ball a little more. It worked, so he let me do it.

Mr. Penick also taught Ben Crenshaw when he was a junior, and in Ben's case he also allowed some liberties. He would let him sway off the ball, which gave Ben a lot of lateral motion with his head. Everybody kept saying he shouldn't do that, but Ben kept doing it and Mr. Penick never changed it, figuring it allowed Ben to hit the ball farther. Ben changed it when he got out on Tour, but I don't know if it was totally with Mr. Penick's blessing.

As I look back now, I suspect Mr. Penick didn't want us to have perfect golf swings. He didn't like the pretty swings much and kept reminding us that "pretty is as pretty does." What he wanted us to do was learn how to *play*.

I once heard a story about another of Mr. Penick's students, Cindy Figg-Currier. She was a really good player at

What he wanted us to do was learn how to play.

KITE AND FRIENDS

*Tom Kite practices
under the watchful
eye of (from left)
LPGA star Sandra
Palmer, Harvey
Penick, caddie
Mike Carrick
and instructor
Chuck Cook.*

He wanted us to figure things out ourselves.

the University of Texas and joined the LPGA Tour full time in 1984. She had always had a very strong grip. Just before she went on Tour Mr. Penick made her grip a little weaker, moving it to where most teachers would have put it in the first place. Asked why he waited until the last minute, just before she was to go on Tour, before he changed her grip, Mr. Penick said, "Had I changed it immediately, she might have been able to hit the ball better but probably wouldn't have developed as good a short game."

In other words, he wanted her to learn how to score before he messed with her swing. In that respect, he is the wisest man I know in golf.

We never got too far from Mr. Penick's watchful eyes. He would tell us, "If you have one bad round, don't worry about it. If you have two bad rounds, go work on it. If you have three bad rounds, call me." He didn't want us to get too far off base, but at the same time he wanted us to be able to figure things out ourselves. That's a good thought for anyone, because the best teacher in the world can't help you if you don't have some idea of what you are trying to do with your golf game. Most of the responsibility falls on the student's shoulders.

Mr. Penick had an incredible influence on golf in Austin and Texas. When I was growing up, Austin had a population of about 300,000, and I'd put it up with any city in the world for the number of single-digit handicap players. Much has been made of the rivalry between Ben and me when we were growing up, but when we were younger there were an awful lot of guys better than we were. It wasn't until we got to the last couple of years of high school and college that we started being able to compete with the rest of the people in town.

A lot of this had to do with the fact that Mr. Penick was there and so many people took lessons from him. There was basically one country club in Austin and everybody at the club was taught by Mr. Penick. And all the other golfers in town, given the opportunity, would take lessons from him. If they couldn't do that, they at least played some golf and listened to somebody who had been taught by Mr. Penick.

I guess Mr. Penick had some influence on about every good player from Texas, male or female, from Ben Hogan, Byron Nelson, Mickey Wright, Kathy Whitworth and Betsy Rawls on down.

Well, I made my first goal, number one on the Lamar Junior High team, but it wasn't a lock. I had some good competition. Then I made number one on the McCallum High School team. I won the Texas high school championship twice. And on my first trip out of Texas, when I was 16, I was a semifinalist in the USGA Junior Championship.

But I wasn't even considered the best player in Austin. By this time, Crenshaw was coming along. Ben went to different schools—O'Henry Junior High and Austin High. And we played each other head to head all the way through. In the early years I probably won more of our matches, mainly because I was two years older. But Ben matured much faster than I did. When I was 15 and he was 13, he probably was more mature physically than I was.

It was a great rivalry. At first we were just a couple of kids playing each other, but in my junior and senior years in high school, one of us would win just about everything around. And we shot some incredibly low scores—61s and 62s and 63s on courses that, while not particularly hard by Tour standards, were considered pretty decent.

But Ben was considered the coming star. Jack Burke Jr. once said Ben was costing himself $100,000 a year by staying an amateur (the purses were a little lower in those days). People used to tell me to be sure to get a good education.

I suppose people thought it inconceivable that two kids could come out of a town that size and make it on Tour. Looking back, I can understand that. But I couldn't understand why they singled me out as the one who wasn't going to make it. I was immature, as most teenagers are, and it hurt. Neither one of us had a perfect swing, but there's no question that Ben's swing looked better than mine. And while I've always been a really good putter, compared with Ben you're never going to look any good. What's obvious to me now is that people think they know what a great player should look like, but in reality great players come in all kinds of packages.

Terry Dill, who was playing the Tour at the time, had moved to Austin and was taking lessons from Mr. Penick. He and Ben and I went out to play one day and Dill said, "I'm really glad that I'm living here in Austin now. This is going to be a tremendous advantage for you. I think I can really help you and Ben with your games." I think Ben shot 65 and I shot 66 or 67 and we both clipped Terry for a few coins. But he later went up to my mother and told her to make sure Tommy got a good education because there was no way he was going to make it on Tour. To this day, Mom really resents that. Moms remember things like that.

Even my dad had some doubts, at least early on. He never really told me not to try for the Tour, but he always encouraged me to do other things, especially to study. He was just afraid I was going to try to make it and not succeed and be hurt. But when I was 16, something happened that eased Dad's mind. He had a good friend name Jock Ducet who lived in Lafayette, Louisiana. Mr. Ducet was a good friend of Lionel and Jay Hebert, who were two of the best players in the game at the time. Each had won a PGA Championship, the only brothers who ever did that. Mr. Ducet invited Dad and me to come to Lafayette and play some golf with the Heberts over the Christmas holidays.

Knowing what I know now, I'm sure they didn't want to play golf with a 16-year-old snotty-nose kid and his dad over the Christmas holidays. They were on their break and one of those "blue northers" had blown in. It was freezing, with the winds whipping around. But we all played. And they gave me some really good advice and memories. I've still got the book of notes I took from them that day.

After the round, both Lionel and Jay told Dad to let me try the Tour. They pointed out that I'd be 22 when I got out of college and I'd find out in three years if I could make it or

Great players come in all kinds of packages.

22

not. I'd still be only 25 and could go on to other things. That was great advice, especially coming from them, and after that Dad never had any reservations about me trying the Tour. I still enjoy being with Lionel and Jay.

I was getting some encouragement from other sources, too. When Ben and I were in college, Betsy Rawls and Judy Kimball came to Austin to play a nine-hole exhibition. Judy and I teamed up against Ben and Betsy. We beat them and I played really well. Afterward, Betsy said there was no doubt in her mind that I could make it on Tour.

In 1971 I got an invitation to play as an amateur in the National Invitation Tournament at Colonial in Fort Worth. I was paired the first two rounds with Billy Maxwell, who was still playing pretty well then and a man who has been very, very nice to me since. After we had played he was quoted in the newspaper as saying, "I haven't seen this Crenshaw kid, but I can guarantee you Tom Kite can make it out here on Tour. That kid's really got some game."

That was encouraging. But I never thought that I wouldn't make it.

At that, I probably had it easier than Ben. People were comparing me with Ben Crenshaw. They were comparing Ben with Jack Nicklaus. I only had to prove I was good enough to play on Tour. Ben had to prove he was another legend.

Choosing a college is a tough decision for an 18-year-old. I was recruited by several schools, but it boiled down to Houston and Texas, and I couldn't make up my mind. Houston was the power in college golf then, and coach Dave Williams was a great recruiter. There are few men I respect more, and anytime he called I would be going to Houston for the rest of the day. But George Hannon, who succeeded Mr. Penick as the coach at Texas, was a good friend, too. I'd known him since I was 13, and I still don't have a better friend today. He kind of let the university sell itself, and I guess it did. I can't really tell you why I went to Texas instead of Houston, but I've never regretted the decision. I guess in the back of my mind I knew that Mr. Penick was in Austin and my family was there, and those might have been the overriding factors.

Freshmen had been made eligible the year before I started at Texas, and I made the team my first year. We had a strong team—guys like Rik Massengale, who went on to play the Tour, Chip Stewart and Dean Overturf were the best. I think I played No. 5, and that was an humbling experience, a cocky kid coming in and finding out there were better players.

Golf is, or should be, full of learning experiences. I remember we went to Houston my freshman year to play in the All-America tournament, really a big deal with bands and cheerleaders and the works. Houston had its live mascot, a cougar named Shasta, at the course, and on my last hole, a par 5, I hooked my second shot and it ended up about 10 feet away from this cat. I probably could have stuck my arm in his mouth and he would have licked me, but I'm just a freshman and don't know that. And of course I'm in Houston territory and I'm either too dumb or too scared to ask the handler to get the cat out of the way. Nobody was around to help me. I had an easy little bump-and-run up to the green, but I got flustered and rushed the shot. I hit it fat and made bogey, and we lost the tournament by a stroke.

I'd like to say I've never rushed a shot since then, but that's not true. There have been a number of other cases where I've played shots when I wasn't ready . . . usually with the same results as when that damned cougar was lying there looking at me. But I do try to get ready before playing a shot.

After Rik and Chip graduated, I played the No. 2 position on the team, behind Dean Overturf, and as a junior I was No. 1. During my senior season Ben and I alternated at No. 1, basically depending on who had won the tournament the week before. We won the Southwest Conference team title in 1971 and 1972, my junior and senior years.

All the while Ben and I were learning from Mr. Penick. He wasn't so much working with our swings as he was teaching us golf. As I look back, most of what he gave us was mental, which I guess is about 95 percent of golf.

I remember one time I wasn't putting particularly well. I had rummaged around in the golf shop and found an ugly old putter. It looked like a piece of junk metal on the end of a shaft. I went to the practice green and putted with it a little bit, and I was still struggling, so I went in and asked Mr. Penick if he would watch me hit some putts. He walked out to the green, and before I could hit a putt he asked, "What is that putter?" I explained that I'd just been fiddling around with it because I hadn't been putting very well. He took it out of my hands and looked at it, put it down and made a stroke or two with it. Then he handed it back to me and said, "Tommy, have you ever seen anybody on the PGA Tour use a putter like this?" I said I really didn't think so. And he said, "Do you think there might be a reason? Now why don't you go get your old putter and then we'll work on your putting."

Don't get too far from home, he was saying. Just know who you are. He always brought you back to earth. He was telling me that I didn't have to change putters to become a good putter. My putting was already good enough. We could correct the flaws through hard work and taking care of the basics.

Mr. Penick always allowed us to experiment with our games, to try something new to see if it would work. He never made us conform to a model. Ben used to like to hit the ball hard, and he could really hit it far for his age. He would hit a big ol' looping hook that would carry a long way and run forever. He would start out with a stance that was just about a perfect width. As he started to hit it better, the stance would get wider and wider, allowing him to sway a little more. But over a period of time that stance would get so wide that pretty soon he couldn't do anything but hit curve balls.

Then he would go back for a lesson after that "third bad round." Mr. Penick would narrow his stance a little and start the cycle all over again. But he let Ben experiment by getting wide because that way he could learn about his own game,

Don't get too far from home . . . just know who you are.

THE MASTER TEACHER

Harvey Penick probably has had more influence on players in Texas, great and otherwise, than any other teacher in history.

learn just how wide he could get to be most effective.

Mr. Penick always encouraged us to hit different shots. We had a set of canisters stuck in the ground about 180 yards out on the practice range. They were used to shoot fireworks on the Fourth of July. There were two big ones about 25 feet apart and three little ones in between, all in a row. I would use the big ones as the left and right sides of the green and one of the little ones as the pin. Then I would try to see how many balls I could hit to a particular pin with different shots. Mr. Penick would come out and say, "Let's see you hit one at the right canister. Start it to the left and fade it in." Then he'd want me to hit it the other way. So I was playing shots while I was practicing instead of just beating balls.

He was a master psychologist. The practice tee was between the ninth green and the 10th tee and players had to walk or drive right by it during a round. A lot of times I'd be working with Mr. Penick as somebody was coming by and he say, "Hey, Mr. Jones, let Tommy show you something. Tommy, show him how you can hit this shot." Now the heat was on. It was a lot tougher with Mr. Jones watching you make the shot than if you were just out there hitting a bucket of balls. I couldn't just drag another ball over if I missed it because Mr. Jones had already gone to the 10th tee.

And Mr. Penick never over-taught. Once he walked up and watched me hit some irons shots. Then he said, "Let's see you hit some drivers." I hit a couple and he said, "You know, I think you're teeing the ball a little high on that driver. Why don't you try teeing it a little lower?" Then he left. It shocked the living daylights out of me. I thought, "That's it? There's got to be more to it than that."

Later that afternoon I went up to him and said, "Mr. Penick, is it anything I did? Did I say something wrong?"

"No," he replied, "your swing is just about where I want it. I didn't see any reason to give you anything that was going to hurt you." He knew I wanted him to give me something, but he made sure it wasn't anything that was going to hurt my game.

That's a good lesson for everybody, teacher and student alike. If it ain't broke, don't fix it.

One of the classic Harvey Penick stories happened before I came on the scene, back when he was still coaching the Texas team. There was a fellow on one of his teams named Billy Munn, a really good player. Back then the conference teams used to play home-and-home matches against each other. Arkansas came to Texas to play at the old Austin Country Club and Billy drew R.H. Sikes. R.H. was the best player in the conference at the time, had a phenomenal short game and, of course, went on to play pretty well on Tour.

Well, Billy played the best round of golf he'd ever had in college. He hit every fairway and hit 17 greens and shot 67, a flawless round. Meanwhile, R.H. is hitting duck hooks and slices and all kinds of garbage shots. He seldom hit a fairway, hit only five or six greens . . . and shot 66 to beat Billy, 1 up.

There was a big, beautiful oak tree down toward the bottom of the putting green with a rock retaining wall around it. As Billy tells the story, after he got beat he went to that old oak to shed some tears and indulge in some self-pity. Mr. Penick walked up and said, "Billy, I just want you to know how proud I was of you out there today. You played a wonderful round of golf, and you should be proud." He started to walk off, then turned around and said, "Oh, one other thing, Billy. Don't ever think for a minute that what you saw out there today was one bit lucky."

If it ain't broke, don't fix it.

In other words, R.H. didn't play a classic round of golf, but he got the job done, and there was no luck involved. I think about all the putts I've seen Ben make, all the 30- and 40-footers, one after the other. And somebody says, "Gosh, he's so lucky." Not for a second is it luck. It's only luck if it happens infrequently. If it happens all the time, there's a pretty good chance it's supposed to happen.

The more I practiced, the more I learned, the luckier I got. Or maybe it wasn't luck. And it was beginning to pay off.

In 1970, at the end of my sophomore year, Ben and I qualified for the U.S. Open at Hazeltine. I missed the cut, but Ben tied with Jim Simons for low amateur honors at 301.

Later that summer I was medalist in the Western Amateur with 273, eight shots ahead of John Mahaffey and Lanny Wadkins. Then I lost to Lanny in the semifinals on the 20th hole.

In September I went to Portland, Oregon, for the U.S. Amateur at the Waverley Country Club. It was a nice little course, and it was really tight. After playing it the first time I called home and told my parents, "This golf course is made for Lanny Wadkins and me." At that time, no amateur could hit it as straight as Lanny or I could, and as it turned out, we were the two who battled down to the end.

I shot 69-67-71 the first three rounds, which at the time was a tournament record, and I still had only a two-stroke lead over Lanny. He caught me by the 14th hole of the final round, and on 15 I hit a good shot but went over the green and made bogey to go a stroke down. We both birdied the next hole, a long, blind par 3. Then we both double-bogeyed the 17th in a comedy of errors. On the last hole, a par 5, Lanny hit his third shot in about 30 feet. I hit mine about eight feet away and thought I might have a chance. Then Lanny drained his putt. I made mine for birdie, too, but I was one stroke too many.

About three weeks later, Lanny, Vinny Giles, Allen Miller and I represented the United States in the World Amateur Team Championship for the Eisenhower Trophy. It was played at the Real Club de la Puerta de Hierro in Madrid, Spain, a good course that measured more than 7,000 yards. Once again it was a learning experience for me, this time about the perils of traveling abroad.

The best three of four scores counted each day, and we were playing consistently. We didn't have a round in the 60s, but my 74 the third day was the highest we shot all week. I had shot 71-70 the first two days, the best on the U.S. team, but everybody was bunched together, and at the end of three rounds we had a nine-stroke lead over South Africa.

That night we went out to dinner. I don't remember what I

It's only luck if it happens infrequently. If it happens all the time, there's a pretty good chance it's supposed to happen.

ate, but I woke up in the middle of the night with food poisoning. The next morning, riding in a taxi with Miller, I was throwing up all the way out. Gus Benedict, a former president of the United States Golf Association and our captain, talked me into trying to play. We had no alternates, so if I dropped out, all three of our remaining scores would have to count.

I threw up again before teeing off, then played the front nine in one over par, just diddly-bumping the ball out there. It was miraculous, considering how I felt. The climb from the ninth green to the 10th tee was straight up a hill, and by the time I got there I thought I was going to pass out. I bogeyed the hole, then went to the 11th tee. We had a wait there, and Gus Benedict told me to go over to the edge of the tee and lie down with an umbrella over me. I did, and the next thing I knew I was in the clubhouse. Joe Dey, then the executive director of the USGA, was there making sure I got enough fluids and whatever else I needed.

I survived and so did the team. Vinny and Lanny each shot 72 and Allen shot 73 and we won by 15 strokes. And I learned to be careful about what I eat abroad. Since then I've learned to be careful about what I eat anywhere. This is not a book on nutrition, but your eating habits can affect your golf or anything else you do. The better your physical condition, the better you can play. Golf is an athletic endeavor, just like every other sport, and you'd better have your body and your mind prepared for it.

I played in my first Masters in 1971 and was second low amateur at 300. That fall I competed for the United States in the Walker Cup Matches at St. Andrews, where we lost for only the third time in history up to then. We had a great team, but in the afternoon on the last day, only Lanny Wadkins and I won our singles matches, and we lost, 13-11.

The next week I lost in the semifinals of the British Amateur to Jim Simons, a Walker Cup teammate and one of my best friends.

In 1972, I returned to the Masters and again finished sec-

Golf is an athletic endeavor ... you'd better have your body and your mind prepared for it.

ond low amateur with a score of 297. I also was second low amateur in the U.S. Open at Pebble Beach, shooting 302 to tie for 19th and finish a stroke behind Simons, who had almost won the Open the year before at Merion.

Two weeks later we played the National Collegiate Athletic Association championship at Fort Myers, Florida, and Texas won it again for the second year in a row. I tied for the individual championship with Crenshaw at 279, and the NCAA had no provisions for a playoff, so we were declared cochampions. Ben had won the title the year before and would win it again in 1973, so at least I didn't interrupt his streak of three straight. But we both would have liked the chance to go at it in a playoff.

Now it was time. I was ready to try the Tour.

CHAPTER 2/ FINDING YOUR SWING

Give luck a chance to happen.

The trick in getting where I am today has been my ability to get in position often enough. If you get there often enough, sooner or later something is going to happen.

Harvey Penick has a great expression: "Give luck a chance to happen." That's where consistency pays off. The more often you put yourself in position to win a golf tournament, the more chances you have to get lucky. I wasn't very far into my professional career when I decided that if I were going to give luck a chance, some changes were needed to become a consistent player—make that a consistently good player.

I turned professional in June of 1972. Because I had been named to the collegiate All-America team and the dinner was in New York, I got a sponsor's exemption into the Westchester Classic. I shot 285, 15 strokes behind Jack Nicklaus, the winner. My first check in golf was for $1,425. I also had an exemption into the USI Classic, thanks to Cuz Mingolla, the tournament sponsor and owner of the Pleasant Valley Country Club. I shot 291 there and won $286.

I was a little nervous. All of a sudden I was playing with

the guys I'd seen and read about for so long, and I was playing courses with conditions I'd never seen. I never had played on bluegrass fairways until I got to Pleasant Valley. I'd never seen shots fly like that before. I quickly saw that I was going to come in contact with many things I'd never experienced before. But I thought I would win a tournament my first year on Tour, which shows how cocky and naïve I was.

In October, I was second by a stroke at the Tour's regional qualifying tournament in Kansas City with a score of 288, and it was on to the final six-round qualifying at Silverado in Napa, California, later that month. I remembered something I'd been told by Lanny Wadkins, who had gone through the school the year before. He talked about trying to win it, rather than just trying to qualify, and I thought that was a pretty good attitude. There were 20 to 25 guys who were going to make it through my school, and I figured if I went there trying to win it rather than just trying to qualify, I had a leeway if I didn't make my goal. That's a pretty good philosophy for any competition. Why enter if you're not trying to win?

I didn't win. I shot 442, 10 over par, for six rounds and finished tied for 10th, which qualified easily. But I really didn't play very well, and it was at that point that I started to see the need to hit the ball higher. I had always hit the ball very low, but I could see that most of the courses I'd be playing on Tour required carries over bunkers and hazards and that I'd have to get the ball in the air a little more. Also, there is not as much wind week in and week out on Tour as we normally see in Texas, where the higher flight just gets eaten up.

The problem was that I didn't know exactly how to get this ball flight. I knew a lot about playing golf, but I didn't know much about the golf swing. I played mostly by feel. Don't get me wrong—playing by feel, with total trust, is the ideal way, the only way to really play your best. But when that feel goes bad, you have to have some fundamental knowledge to fall back on so the slumps are of short duration. It's impossible to know what you're doing wrong if you don't know what you were doing right. I didn't, so it was tough for me to check myself now that I wasn't so near to Harvey Penick.

There were still two tournaments left on the schedule after I got my card. I failed to qualify at Hilton Head, but I made it at Walt Disney World. I shot 67 in the first round and was up near the lead. I don't remember where I finished, but I made the cut, which qualified me for the Los Angeles Open, the first tournament of 1973. In my first three tournaments as a professional, I had won a total of $2,582. But it was a start.

Over the winter, Mr. Penick cautioned me about playing on the West Coast. At that time there were still a lot of club professionals playing the Tour in the winter, guys like Gene Borek and Tom Nieporte and other good players. So the competition was strong, the fields were full and there weren't many qualifying spots available. I think Mr. Penick was afraid I'd have trouble qualifying and didn't want my confidence shattered.

But wild horses couldn't have kept me away from Los Angeles. I finished 17th there and made the cut in the next tournament, but I missed at Tucson. The tournament was at Tucson National, where the NCAA championship had been played my junior year. I didn't play worth beans then and I didn't play it worth beans as a professional.

I missed qualifying for the Bob Hope Classic the next month—I was a pitiful Monday qualifier—but back then they had a satellite tournament called The Hope of Tomorrow. It was played at Palm Desert Country Club, and I shot 66-65-67—198 to win it. That got me into the Hope the next year and into the next event at San Diego, where I finished tied for 22nd. I never had to qualify again. I had a couple of sponsor's exemptions and I made the cut in every tournament I played.

Bob Day, a graduate of the University of Connecticut who wanted to take a year off before he started working, began caddieing for me early in the season. I told him that I didn't

> I hate planning to play golf on the weekend and then not being able to.

know how things would go, that we probably would make some cuts and miss some. After the last tournament of the year at Walt Disney World, Bob said, "Tom, everything has been great and I've really enjoyed it. But you lied to me. You said we would make some cuts and miss some, and we never missed a cut." I still don't miss cuts—at least not very many. I hate planning to play golf on the weekend and then not being able to do so.

At the end of the year I had won $54,270 and finished 56th on the money list, which exempted me for 1974. And I was named Rookie of the Year by *Golf Digest.* But I still had a lot of work to do on my swing.

I had met Bob Toski during the Florida portion of the Tour and had begun working with him. It was hard for me to get home to see Mr. Penick, and Bob was spending a lot of time on Tour as a commentator for Hughes Sports Television. We became great friends, and he's still like a second father to me. He gave me the direction I needed. He defined the golf swing for me. I had always lined up to the right of the target with the ball back in my stance, which meant my shoulders and hips would be too level. Then I would take the club quickly to the inside with a flat, wristy motion, swing way to the right of my target and hit that low hook. It worked a lot of the time but it was not the shot for the courses on Tour. I had to do something to change the flight.

Toski set my left hip and shoulder higher and my right side lower at address and had me line up slightly left of my target. That forced my backswing to go straighter back and made my swing more upright. That corrected my major problem and let me hit the ball higher. It was something I'd always been trying to do but couldn't with the alignment I had.

Bob gave me a lot of good advice. There were some things I didn't understand about his teaching. I didn't know enough about the golf swing to be able to understand everything he was talking about. I'm only now beginning to realize how smart he is.

I kept bombarding Bob with questions. I wanted to learn

Toski gave me the direction I needed.

Edison now knew 700 things that didn't work and he didn't have to try them again.

everything I could about the golf swing. I've always been inquisitive, and I've tried to get as much information as I could from people who I thought knew something about golf. When I was growing up, Mr. Penick was there and I totally trusted him. I totally trust him now and I still work with him. There's never been a time that I haven't worked with him. But when I got out on Tour, I became exposed to more and different ideas, and I listened. I still do. I don't listen to just anybody. But if I hear somebody and like what he's talking about, I'll try hit ideas. I've talked golf with a lot of teachers, including Mr. Penick, Bob Toski, Jim Flick, the late Davis Love, Peter Kostis, Chuck Cook, Bill Strasbaugh, Dennis Satyshur, John Rhodes and others. And I talk to the players on Tour. If I see something I like in their swings, I'm not hesitant to ask what they're working on and try it in my own game. So many guys out here have been so good to me. Dave Stockton, for example, has been very helpful with his ideas on putting.

I suppose I haven't been very loyal in my search for knowledge, in that I talk to all these different people rather than trusting my game to just one. It's almost like I have to get a second or third opinion, just as you go to a doctor who gives you a diagnosis. You respect him, but you want another opinion. You're not necessarily doubting him. You're just confirming—or not confirming—his diagnosis.

There is nothing wrong with experimenting, for me or for you. The story is told about Thomas Edison trying 700 different things to find the right material for the filament in his light bulb. Somebody asked him if all that testing discouraged him. He said, no, that now he knew 700 things that didn't work and he didn't have to try them again.

You've probably tried a new driver, a new wedge, a new putter, or you will if you play golf for any length of time. If the new club works, you keep it in your bag. If not, you replace it. If the new swing thought works, you keep using it. If it doesn't, you go back to your old one or something else. That's the way I've approached my golf swing. If it works, I'll do it. If it doesn't, I won't.

But you can overload the computer. You have to be able to sort it all out. The key to experimenting is that *you must always know where you are so you can go back*. Don't get lost making changes. It's easy to overdo things. You might make a half-inch change in your stance, for example, and it feels pretty good. Pretty soon to get that same feeling you move another inch, then two inches, and after a while you've over-cooked it and it isn't working anymore. So you have to be able to go back to where you started. It's good to have a home base, and having a kind, educated instructor at home makes it that much better. Don't wander around in a maze of changes until you are totally confused.

The changes Toski suggested for my swing were just the first of many I've made. The golf swing is not a static entity. It changes as the knowledge changes, as the body changes, as the particular desired shot pattern changes. My swing probably has changed every year, and it looks a lot different today than it did 20 years ago, or even two years ago. For me it has been a series of steps forward and steps back and steps forward again. I'm not sure I had a real clear road map of where I was going, so my swing probably didn't improve as quickly as I'd have liked it to.

Sometimes I feel that I'm just now learning to swing the club as efficiently as possible and am able to hit the quality shots that I want. My ball striking is better than it has ever been, but it has taken a long time. And I'm sure I'm not through learning. I'd better not be.

Mr. Penick helped me learn to score, and that's by far the most important thing in this game. But I wanted to make sure I understood the golf swing, too. That's a good order of preference for anybody. Learn to play golf, then work on improving your swing. Just remember that takes some time and effort.

I'm going to give you the fundamentals and the swing technique as I see them now. But these should just be guide-lines. Adapt them to fit your body and your preferences.

> The key to experimenting is that you must always know where you are so you can go back.

There is no right or wrong way to play golf. Whatever works and whatever you have confidence in is what you should use.

SETTING UP TO THE BALL

The preparations you make before hitting a golf shot are maybe more important than the swing itself. Your grip, posture, stance, alignment and the other setup fundamentals dictate what probably will happen in your swing. They may vary according to your physical build and what you're trying to do with your shot, but the swing follows as a cause-and-effect relationship, and if you don't devote some time to the setup fundamentals and make them consistent with your swing philosophy, chances are you're not going to make good swings consistently.

How to hold the club. Mr. Penick has an expression: "If you have a bad grip you don't really want a good swing." What he means is that a classic golf swing requires a classic grip. Sam Snead has a classic golf swing and a classic grip. Paul Azinger has a strong grip, with both hands turned to the right. If Azinger swung like Snead, he would hook the ball badly. So Azinger has to make some compensations in his swing to hit the ball as well as he does—and he does hit it well. Maybe he doesn't have a classic swing, but it's effective. Mr. Penick's point is that you cannot expect to have a classic swing with a less-than-classic grip. And, unless you have the talent of a Paul Azinger, it's better to start with a good grip and make your swing as simple and free of compensations as possible.

The grip is your only connection to the golf club. It establishes the relationship between your body and the clubface and dictates how you must swing to hit a decent shot.

The first chapter of practically every book on instruction deals with the grip. But it's amazing the number of amateurs we play with in pro-ams who apparently started the book in Chapter 2. Please don't skip the next few pages.

Your hands should be in a neutral position, much like they

> If you have a bad grip, you don't really want a good swing.

are when they are hanging at your sides, because that's the position to which they naturally want to return at impact. There should be no twisting or turning of the hands when they are put on the club. They have to work together so that neither controls or overpowers the other.

The club should be held in the palm of the left hand, running diagonally from under the heel pad to the base of the fingers. It should be held in the fingers of the right hand, with the right forefinger slightly crooked. Your left thumb should fit into the groove between the pads of the right hand. The left thumb also should be "long" or stretched out flat on the shaft. This gives you more support at the top of the swing. You ought to almost completely cover the left thumb with your right hand.

Each thumb should be slightly to the opposite side of the shaft—the right thumb a little left of center, the left thumb slightly to the right. If you don't get the thumbs a little bit off center, then you're not putting yourself in control of the club.

The most common grip is called the Vardon or overlapping grip in which the little finger of the right hand overlaps or is hooked around the forefinger of the left. I use the interlocking grip, with the little finger of the right hand and the forefinger of the left entwined or hooked together. That's because I have short, thick fingers. Jack Nicklaus, who also has small hands, uses that grip, too.

If I had it to do over again, I'd probably try the ten-finger grip, in which all your fingers are on the club, the little finger of the right hand snug against the forefinger of the left. That would give me a little more control. Because my hands are small, they tend to get too bunched together. I wish I could stretch them down the club more like players with big hands. The ten-finger grip is excellent for juniors and those with small hands, because more of the hands are on the club and there is more control. The only drawback is that the hands are not as unified. Players like Bob Rosburg and Art Wall have used the ten-finger grip very successfully as

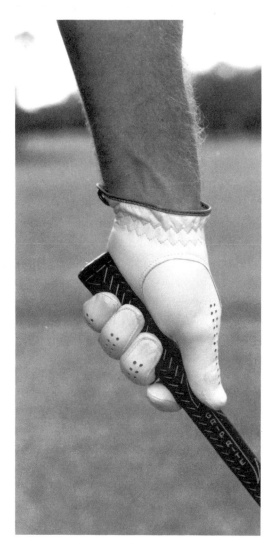

LEFT HAND: IN THE PALM

The club is held in the palm of the left hand. The handle runs diagonally from under the heel pad to the base of the fingers (left). The thumb is placed slightly to the right side of the handle.

LEFT THUMB IS 'LONG'

Above is how the back of the left hand grip should look. The left thumb should be "long" or laid down the shaft (left) to provide more support at the top of the swing.

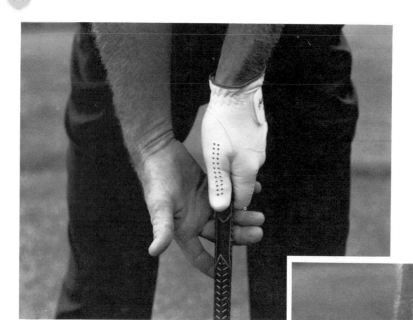

RIGHT HAND: IN THE FINGERS

The handle runs across the base of the right-hand fingers, which then close around the club. The left thumb fits in the groove between the pads of the right hand (right). With the interlocking grip shown here, the forefinger of the left hand and the little finger of the right are intertwined.

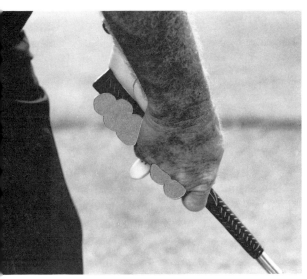

COMPLETED GRIP

Here are four looks at the completed grip. The hands are placed on the club in basically the same position as they hang naturally from your shoulders. The pressure should be in the last three fingers of the left hand and the middle two fingers of the right (above and top right). The right thumb sits slightly to the left side of the shaft and the Vs formed by the thumbs and forefingers point approximately just inside the right shoulder.

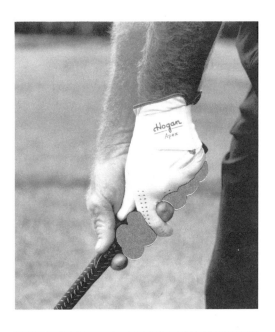

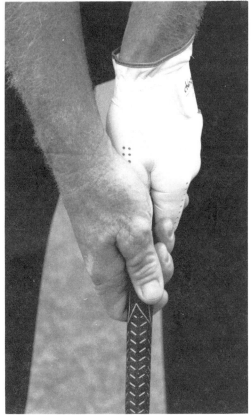

professionals.

No matter which grip style you use, the pressure points are in the last three fingers of the left hand and the middle two fingers of the right. For the purpose of swinging a golf club, you could cut off your right thumb and forefinger.

The club must be held securely. I want to hold it as tightly as possible without creating any tension in my forearms. If I feel tension there, I know I'm in trouble. A good test is to pick up a club and have a friend try to tug it out of your hands. He shouldn't be able to. You should exert just enough pressure not to let him. But your arms should still be relaxed and tension-free. In my clinics I relate to the grip pressure you use when you're eating with a spoon or fork. You will not drop the utensil or overcontrol it, else you will miss your mouth completely.

Obviously, your grip pressure is going to be lighter for a six-inch putt than for a full drive. And your pressure will increase instinctively from address to the top and through impact. It doesn't take much pressure to hold a 13-ounce club when it's static. But when it's moving at 100 miles an hour at the bottom of your swing, it effectively weighs a lot more and you'd better hold on. But there should be no sudden change in your grip pressure. It should increase gradually, and it will, without your worrying about it. You shouldn't feel any change, but the motion of your swing will cause it to increase. I've never seen anybody throw a club down the fairway making a golf swing because he was gripping it too lightly.

The neutral position, as your hands hang at your sides, should just be a starting point. You can play successfully with slight variations in each direction, but you have to do something to compensate. If you have a weak or "slice" grip, both hands turned more to the left, then you have to release the club much faster with your hands, arms or shoulders . . . or some combination. Johnny Miller has both hands turned very much to the left and he releases the club with a lot of hand action. Curtis Strange has a relatively weak left hand

You will not drop the utensil or overcontrol it, else you will miss your mouth completely.

position and he releases the club a lot with his shoulders and upper body.

If you have what is known as a strong or "hook" grip, with both hands turned to the right, then you're going to have to force them to come back to impact in that position. So you'll have to make some compensating move with your body or arms to do that. You also see less hand action among good players with strong grips, because they don't want the clubface to turn over. Azinger and Lee Trevino, for example, have very strong grips. They set the club at the top and use a tremendous clearing of the left hip to make sure the clubface is not closed at impact. Consequently they both play fades.

In other words, if you have a slice grip, you'd better have a hook swing. If you have a hook grip, you'd better have a slice swing. Bruce Lietzke has a hook grip and a slice swing. Billy Casper, in his prime, had a hook grip but faded the ball with a slice swing. Ben Hogan hooked the ball badly early in his career with a flat, inside-to-outside swing path, but when he rebuilt his swing he set his left hand on the club in a weak or slice position. He still had a flat swing with a strong release, but now he could fade the ball . . . actually, what he did was hit it very, very straight.

What you don't want is a hook grip and a hook swing or, as is the case with many amateur players, a slice grip and a slice swing. A lot of amateur players I see have grips that are too weak, especially in the left hand. When the left hand is on the club in too weak a position, the right hand tends to take over and control the swing from the top. So they tend to come over the top and swing from outside to inside, cutting across the ball from right to left. They've now combined a slice grip with a slice swing and—surprise, surprise!—they get a slice.

These players need a stronger left hand grip, because it promotes a flatter swing. That helps you come at the ball a little more from the inside, which promotes a draw and a stronger shot. Just make sure the right hand doesn't get turned too far to the right, because that can cause problems.

What you don't want is a hook grip and a hook swing or a slice grip and a slice swing.

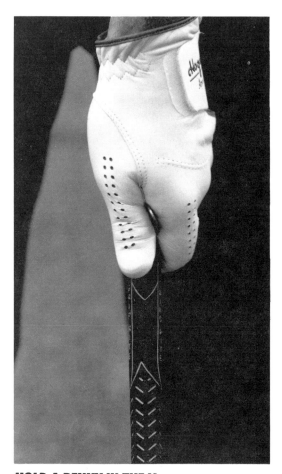

HOLD A PENNY IN THE Vs

For better control of the club, the thumbs and forefingers of each hand should be pinched together enough that you can hold a penny in the Vs formed by each. This has to do with position, not pressure. The pressure is in the last three fingers of the left hand and the middle two fingers of the right.

DIFFERENT GRIPS

Shown are three different ways to hold the club and unify the hands—the interlocking grip, in which the left forefinger and right little finger are intertwined; the overlapping or Vardon grip, in which the little finger of the right lies over or hooks around the forefinger of the left; and the ten-finger grip, in which all the fingers are on the club, the little finger of the right sitting snugly against the forefinger of the left.

INTERLOCKING

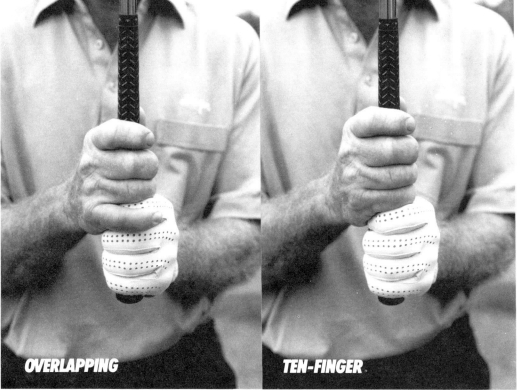

OVERLAPPING

TEN-FINGER

There's a trend on Tour now toward a stronger left hand grip, but for a different reason. The professionals want the flatter, stronger swing, but they want to guard against a hard hook. So they just block the ball and eliminate the left side of the course.

The point is, it's good if it works, if it produces the shots that allow you to shoot the score you are capable of. Experiment with various grip positions and styles and see what matches your swing style and your physique. Never be afraid to try different things.

> It's good if it works, if it produces the shots that allow you to shoot the score you are capable of.

I've used the interlocking grip right from the start, probably because my dad did. He has short, thick fingers, too, although I don't know how he came upon the grip. After my round with Jay and Lionel Hebert, back when I was 16, they recommended that I try the Vardon overlapping grip. They felt it was the preferred grip and they wanted me to try it. So the next summer I did, for a month or so. I found that with my fingers I couldn't hold on to the club as well, so I went back to the interlock and have used it ever since. But the point is, I did try it. Never hesitate to experiment. If something works, incorporate it into your game. If it doesn't, well, like Edison, that's something you don't have to try anymore.

A grip change—any change, for that matter—is a traumatic thing for most players. It just feels awkward at first. But don't let that scare you away. In a few days it will feel good. And you don't have to hit 1,000 balls a day to make that happen. In the case of the grip, especially, just hold the club in your hands while you're taking a break at the office, or while you're at home in the evening watching television, and in a short time it will feel like you've been holding it that way all your life.

How to stand to the ball. Your address position involves your posture, the width of your stance and weight distribution, aiming the clubface and aligning the body.

Posture is critical in making a good golf swing. The most

important thing here is to create a spine angle, a tilt to the spine, that you are able to maintain throughout the swing. To do that you must be in balance, bent properly from the hips and with some flex in your knees. A good guideline here is that if someone were to push you gently, either forward or backward, you would be able to maintain your balance. Bend from your hips and flex your knees so that your hands are hanging almost straight down, maybe just slightly extended, and your club is soled or sitting on the ground properly with neither the toe nor the heel too high in the air. As you bend from the hips, keep your spine straight (but not rigid). It's hard to have an angle with a curved line. Your spine does curve normally, of course, but feel there's a straight line running from the base of the spine to the top of your head. This also keeps your head straight and your eyes in position to look squarely at the ball. In my case, I look at the ball through the center of my glasses. If my head were drooping, I couldn't do that.

Your weight should be distributed between the balls and heels of your feet and equally distributed between the two feet. You should be able to tap your heels and wiggle your toes.

At this point you have counterbalanced your weight. You should be able to draw a vertical line from the back of your shoulders through your knees to the balls of your feet. Now you are in balance. Your body tilt, knee flex and arm hang are compatible and you are in position to make a dynamic move with the hips and legs and swing without your arms running into your body. And you will be able to maintain your spine angle throughout the swing.

Remember, the amount you bend over will depend on what club you have in your hands—more with a 9-iron, less with a driver. But you don't have to worry about that. The length of the club, if it is soled properly, will determine the correct posture for you.

If you stand too straight, your posture is too passive, your knees are too stiff and you're not going to be able to make a

A constant spine angle produces consistency.

move with any real speed. If you bend over too far, you have to flex your knees more. This tends to create tension that also reduces potential speed.

Mike Campbell, an assistant coach at Texas under Darrell Royal, used to say that one reason Earl Campbell, the Long-horns' All-American fullback, was so difficult to take down was that he could run so low and with so much power with his knees flexed. He could keep them pumping and always get three or four more yards after he was hit. Unfortunately, few of us are as strong as Earl Campbell. If we get our knees flexed too much, we can't move our legs well enough to support a strong swing.

Also, bending over too far makes it difficult to maintain a consistent spine angle through the swing. Fuzzy Zoeller and Hubert Green both have their spines so tilted at address that they have to raise up during the swing. Julius Boros used to do the same thing. Fuzzy's head actually rises three or four inches from where it started. I've had doctors tell me that could be one reason he has so much trouble with his back. If he kept his spine angle constant, there might be less strain.

More important (at least from a golf standpoint), a constant spine angle creates consistency. Al Geiberger probably has the most consistent spine angle of anybody I've seen, and there have been few more consistent players in history.

Once you've assumed the correct posture position with your hands on the club, your right shoulder will be set slightly lower than your left. This is natural because your right hand is lower than your left on the club. I wouldn't want you to exaggerate it. Some players do set up with their right sides too high, but that usually is more a function of a grip that is too weak or turned to the left. If your grip is basically correct, your right side will be slightly lower.

The width of your stance has a lot to do with the length and shape of your swing. A good rule of thumb is that your stance with a 5-iron, measured at the insides of your heels, should be the width of your shoulders. But there are many variations. The wider your stance, the wider and lower or flatter your swing is going to be. A wider stance inhibits the hip turn. A narrower stance encourages more turning of the hips and a longer, more vertical swing.

For example, Paul Azinger clears his hips a tremendous amount on the forward swing. He has to have a relatively narrow stance, maybe as narrow as anybody since Bobby Jones, to allow him to turn as quickly as he does. Curtis Strange, on the other hand, has a very wide stance and a wide, lateral swing. Hal Sutton and Peter Jacobsen have similar swings and both have wide stances.

Your body build also has something to do with it. Davis Love III has a wide stance, but he's tall and slim and supple. He can take a wide stance and still make an enormous turn. Bob Toski is shorter but still has a wide stance, because he's very supple. Al Geiberger is tall and supple with a narrow stance, and he's an advocate of turning his hips both back and through.

I've changed my philosophy a little bit over the years. When I first came on Tour I had a very wide stance. In trying to gain some distance and increase my turn, I made my stance narrower. After a period of time my bigger hip turn allowed my swing to get too long, so now I've gone back to a wider stance. That shortens my swing and makes it wider and flatter. It also helps me stay in balance and move through the ball better. I'm sure you've heard the old saying that two aspirin can cure a headache but the whole bottle will kill you. Well, we all have to be careful with the changes we make in our swings.

You have to find your own ideal stance width. If you are bigger and taller, you may need a wider stance. I'd say that if you are to err, a wider stance would be better than a narrow one because balance is so important. Basically, you don't want to fall down. You want to be able to maintain your balance while making a full swing. Experiment to see what is right for you.

Your stance instinctively will narrow as the club gets shorter. I've never seen anybody stand as wide for a wedge

We all have to be careful with the changes we make in our swings.

THE STANCE

WEIGHT BALANCED

At address, set up with the weight distributed equally, left and right. The right shoulder will be slightly lower than the left, because the right hand is below the left on the club. The right foot is square or turned out just slightly. The left foot can be turned out more to allow a faster hip-turn coming through.

SET THE SPINE ANGLE

*Bend from the hips and keep the spine angle straight from the
lower back to the top of the shoulders, then maintain that
angle throughout the swing. The weight should be counterbalanced along a vertical line from the back of the shoulders
through the knees to the balls of the feet.*

Good players will combine things that work.

shot as they do for a driver. You don't need as much speed, as much turn, for the shorter shots, so you don't need as much support from your base. That will happen instinctively.

The angle of your feet is important. The more square or perpendicular to the target line you set your right foot, the more you tend to restrict your hip turn on the backswing and the easier it is to turn your hips coming through. The more you angle the right foot out, to the right, the bigger hip turn you can make, but then it's a little harder to get cleared on the forward swing. The same with the left foot. Angling it to the left helps restrict the hip turn on the backswing and allows a faster turn coming through. The squarer the left foot, the bigger the backswing turn you can get.

For full shots, I set the right foot reasonably square, toed out just a little. My left foot is angled much more to the left for the reasons I just mentioned—I'm trying to restrict my backswing hip turn and turn faster coming forward, which I'll discuss more later on. Experiment with the angles of your feet to find out what it does to your swing.

How to aim the shot. If I were going to teach somebody the ideal way to play golf, I'd have him or her aim the clubface squarely at the target with the body aligned parallel to the target line but left of it—parallel left, in other words. The interesting thing is that nobody out here on Tour plays that way. Lee Trevino and Paul Azinger play from very open stances, lined up to the left of the target, because each plays with a hook grip and a slice swing. They either cut or block the ball back to the target.

The opposite is true with guys like Sam Snead and Gary Player and Johnny Miller, who set up to the right. They are so supple and turn so well that they can align their bodies that way and still square the clubface.

Good players will combine things that work. They might line up left or right, but then they will make a swing that will get the ball back to the target.

I remember hearing a story about somebody who went up

to Snead and told him he was not lined up correctly. Sam said, "No, if you were standing in my stance, *you* would not be lined up correctly, but *I* am lined up correctly." That's because his alignment was compatible with his swing and the ball was going where he wanted it to go.

If you put Snead in Trevino's stance and Trevino in Snead's stance and had them hit drivers, their balls would end up 175 yards apart on opposite sides of the target. Sam would hit it way left and Lee would hit it way right. Their alignment would be incompatible with their swings.

Some years ago Mickey Wright and Betsy Rawls gave a clinic in Austin, and during it Mickey made the comment that you should never practice without a target. Afterward, Mr. Penick questioned her about that remark. They came to the conclusion that if you are hitting solid shots and getting the ball flight you want, and if the ball isn't going to the target, you are lined up wrong.

So don't make your alignment dictate the ball flight. Let the ball flight dictate your alignment. The majority of the best players do not line up perfectly square to the target. They line up in a way that accommodates their shots. My suggestion would be to work on the things that produce the ball flight you want, then adjust your alignment so your ball goes to the target. You can do it by trial and error. Go out and hit some balls. If the ball is going fairly consistently in a certain direction and that doesn't happen to be your target, then you are lined up incorrectly to accommodate your shots.

It's really only important that the clubface be square at impact, but that's probably easier to do if it's square at address. Most players on Tour play with a square-to-slightly-open clubface at address. The good player will tend to draw the ball from an open clubface at address, because he instinctively rotates it back to square and closing through impact. Jack Nicklaus, who plays with a slightly open clubface, once said he sets up so he can't hook the ball, then he tries to hook it. The result is a powerful shot that fades . . . very slightly.

If you are getting the ball flight you want and the ball isn't going to the target, you are lined up wrong.

A line drawn across the top of your forearms or across your shoulders determines where you are lined up.

But many players below Tour caliber will slice if the clubface is open at address because they will try to square it up with their shoulders. Then they cut across the ball and get a big banana. So it's best to set the clubface square, aiming it directly down your starting line.

Then set your body perpendicular to the clubface or parallel to the line on which you want the ball to start. The shoulder and forearm alignment is more important than that of the feet. A line drawn across the top of your forearms or across your shoulders (you can have somebody lay a club across them) pretty much determines where you are lined up. It's really not important where your feet are aligned. Your feet can be pointing almost anywhere. If you look at Snead, I think you'll find his shoulders are not pointing as much to the right as his feet are. Trevino's shoulders are not pointing as much to the left as his feet are.

Look at the good hitters in baseball. Their feet might be in any position, but their shoulders and hips are usually square as they stand at the plate. So, after you aim your clubface, work to get your shoulders and forearms square.

You might want your feet in different positions for certain reasons. If you close your stance, dropping your right foot back, you can get your right side out of the way easier and make a bigger backswing turn. An open stance, your left foot dropped back, curtails your backswing and allows you to clear your hips faster on the forward swing. This is especially effective on a short shot, where a big turn is not as important and you actually are trying to restrict the backswing a little bit.

And, of course, you want to close your stance and aim right for a deliberate hook. Open your stance and aim left for a deliberate slice.

I hear and read a lot about using the intermediate target as an aiming device—stand behind the ball and pick out a spot, a leaf or divot or whatever, between you and the ball in line with your target. Nicklaus is a great advocate of it. Frankly, it's never worked for me. The intermediate spot always looks like it's right of where I'm supposed to be aiming. Golf is a game played from the side, so aiming is one of the hardest things to do. But aiming from behind is totally foreign to what you're going to be doing when you're over the ball. I've always felt that you could see everything from beside the ball that you could see from behind it. But you might want to try the intermediate target. If it works for Jack, it could work for you.

Your weight should be equally distributed between your feet. In the golf swing you must transfer your weight toward the target on the forward swing to hit with any power. The longer the shot, the more the weight transfer—your weight shift is much greater with a driver than with a pitching wedge. Therefore it's important to get the weight to the right side on the backswing so you can drive to the left on the forward swing.

Peter Jacobsen has taken batting practice with the Oakland A's and has talked with Mark McGwire. He thinks the baseball and golf swings are similar, except that the baseball hitters don't have time for a backswing and the planes are different. They actually lean toward the back foot as they stand in the box so they can transfer their weight quickly forward as the pitch comes in. But in the golf swing you have more time (the ball won't move) to shift back and through, to build up centrifugal force and momentum, so a 50-50 balance at address is a good place to start.

How to position the ball. The position of the ball in relation to your stance is one of the most important and most overlooked fundamentals in golf. And it's really quite simple, if you pay attention.

Your ball position determines to a great extent if your shoulders are parallel to your target line. If you play the ball too far forward, your shoulders will tend to aim left at address. If the ball is too far back in your stance, it will take your shoulder alignment to the right.

With a driver, I like to see the ball positioned off the left

Your ball position determines to a great extent if your shoulders are parallel to your target line.

WIDTH VARIES WITH CLUB

The stance width varies with the club. It should be slightly wider than shoulder-width with the driver, measured from the insides of the heels. It should be shoulder width with the 5-iron and progressively narrower as the clubs get shorter. With the driver, the ball is positioned off the left heel or the left instep. For all other clubs, play it an inch or two farther back in the stance.

DRIVER   5-IRON   WEDG

DRIVER

5-IRON

CLUB DETERMINES TILT

How much a player bends from the hips is determined by the length of the club. The upper body will be more erect with the driver, tilting progressively more as the club gets shorter. The arms hang basically straight down, reaching only slightly with the longer clubs.

WEDGE

Nowadays you have to play the ball in the air.

instep. I know that is probably farther forward than you have been told in the past, but having the ball forward encourages you to move through to the left side. With the fairway woods and iron clubs, position the ball about an inch inside the left heel. I don't advocate moving the ball back in your stance for the shorter clubs, because that moves your shoulder alignment to the right and inhibits your drive through the ball.

As your club gets shorter and your stance narrows, it will look like you are playing the ball more toward the center of your stance, but that's only because you are moving your right foot toward the ball. Its position in relation to the left foot stays the same.

In days past, players played the ball farther back because the golf courses were firmer and allowed for the low, bounce-up shot. Nowadays the courses are watered to excess and bunkered to excess, so you have to play the ball in the air more.

When the Austin Country Club moved across town to its new Pete Dye course on the west side, Mr. Penick was asked if he had taught for all those years at this new facility how it would have affected his teaching. Mr. Penick said he would have taught his students to play the ball farther forward, because the golf course and the maintenance dictated that the ball be played higher.

Ideally, you should address the ball with the center of your clubface, but I see a lot of deviation from that on Tour. I set the heel of the club next to the ball, so for me to hit the ball on the center of the face I've got to swing inside of where I started. That's much better than addressing the ball with the toe. Nobody on Tour does that, because that forces you to swing outside your starting point and creates an over-the-top or outside-in move that makes you cut across the ball.

Fuzzy Zoeller, for example, goes to the extreme. He doesn't even address the ball. He literally bounces the club out beyond it before he starts his swing. He says that reminds him to return the club from the inside. Actually, it lowers his spine angle and *forces* him to raise up and swing from the inside. You can't argue with Fuzzy's success. He's always been one of our top players, and if he hadn't had a bad back he would have been phenomenal, one of the greatest who ever played the game. He has a great attitude, especially in the major championships. But his swing would be very difficult to duplicate for most players, and I really wouldn't recommend his method.

Julius Boros has much the same kind of action at address. So does Frank Beard. That only proves what I've been saying all along—there's a lot of room in golf for a person to be his own individual. I like to see people do whatever produces the best score, not necessarily what makes the prettiest swing. Remember that nothing about the swing is carved in stone. Experiment to find what is best for you.

How to waggle the club. Like everything else in golf, the waggle is an individual thing. It is simply a movement of the club that should reduce tension and prepare you to start your swing.

When I was a kid, I used to "milk" the club. I'd set the clubhead on the ground behind the ball and leave it there. I'd put my hands on it and just kind of keep pumping them— open and close, open and close—until I was ready to swing. When my dad and I visited the Heberts that one winter, Lionel told me right then to quit doing that. He told me to put my hands on the club and leave them there. He said you have to have a waggle, you have to move the clubhead. This was back when Doug Sanders was in his prime and was one of the best players in the game. Lionel pointed out that Doug was the only good player who did not waggle the clubhead. He milked the club like I was doing, and he jiggled his feet. If you don't waggle, you have to do something to get your swing in motion. Consequently, Doug had a difficult time getting his swing started and could stand over the ball forever.

Of course, if you milk the club, you have to leave the clubhead on the ground. If it were in the air, you'd drop it every time you re-gripped it. Lionel said that if Doug had learned a waggle, he would have played faster and possibly lasted longer.

This was the first I'd heard about a waggle. Mr. Penick had never said anything to me about it. When I got home, I asked him. He said players waggle in different ways. Some waggle with their hands and arms, some waggle with their feet. But he said most do waggle the club back and forth, and he didn't have any problem with me doing that.

Some players and instructors will tell you that the waggle previews your swing. I guess in one sense it does—the shorter the shot, the smaller the waggle; the longer the shot, the bigger the waggle, in most cases. Bob Toski taught me to waggle the club with my hands, moving the club back and forward along my takeaway line with my left arm staying relatively still, and that's the way I do it today. That's what is meant by a preview of the swing. But I see many variations. Johnny Miller waggles the club straight up and down. Jack Nicklaus has kind of an up-and-down movement, and you can see that he's loosening up his arms as he does this.

I've looked at old films of Ben Hogan and Sam Snead and some other players of that era, and part of their waggles consisted of folding their arms and pulling the club upward as they addressed the ball. This would certainly loosen the tension in the arms.

The waggle is usually followed by some kind of forward press, the final move that initiates the backswing. Again, this is done in many different ways. Gary Player has a pronounced kicking in of the right knee toward the target before he starts back. So did Hogan. So does Toski and Paul Azinger and a lot of others. Nicklaus leans slightly to his left and then begins his backswing. I tap my left toes and make a slight forward movement of my hands before I start back. I've tried the knee kick, but when I do that it exaggerates my press and throws my hands and clubface way open. Maybe just a little rock with the whole body would be ideal. In any case, this is the move that triggers the start of the swing.

SWINGING THE CLUB

There is much more to hitting an effective golf shot than just swinging the club. You have to visualize the shot and you should have a consistent preshot routine that will prepare you for making the swing. You also have to be prepared mentally and emotionally, and I'll discuss that in a separate chapter. For now, let me give you my ideas on the mechanics of the golf swing.

How to make the swing. My definition of a good golf swing is one that is capable of hitting the ball the required distance with accuracy . . . and one that repeats. A good golf swing is one that constantly produces low scores. A pretty golf swing may or may not do that, so a pretty swing is not too important to me. It may be important to some teachers who are teaching swing. I'd like to teach you golf.

There always has been a great debate among teachers and players over which is the most important in the golf swing, the arms or the body. I've gone through all stages in trying to learn the swing, and my conclusion is that it should all happen together.

I really like the term "one piece," which means that the club, your arms, your upper body and your feet and legs all start back together. To me, it almost feels like the body swings the club back. I know from looking at films and videos and high-speed sequences that the arms start moving first and then the body kicks in. But if your thought is to swing the arms back first, they tend to break away from the body and you can get a big arm swing with very little body turn—both out of sync with each other.

Try this. Stand at address and, without taking a backswing, go to your finish position. You instinctively will go there with your body, not just with your arms. Feel how your body turns through and your arms are carried to the finish position. You'll be in perfect balance. This is the feeling you should strive for throughout the swing. The body turns and the arms keep pace. The bigger the body turn and the faster

A good golf swing is one that constantly produces low scores.

63

it turns, the longer and faster the arm swing.

So the common error is having way too much arm swing and not nearly enough body action. I see too many amateurs who swing their arms but don't turn their shoulders or their hips. As a result, they lift their arms, but there is no rotation to their swings. They don't turn enough on the backswing to be able to make a good forward swing into the ball.

Somebody who is flexible might be able to get away with this. His arm swing may pull his shoulders and body around. But that doesn't seem to happen with most golfers. I've heard the argument that you can turn your shoulders without swinging your arms, and I guess that's true. But I believe swinging the arms is instinctive in golf. If you are going to move the ball, you have to swing your arms back and swing them down again. I have never seen anybody turn his body without swinging his arms. The problem is getting your body to turn enough to support that swinging of your arms. Your arms and hands have farther to go, but they can move faster. The big muscles of your back don't have the suppleness or range of motion that your arms do. The good news is that they don't have to, because they're turning at the center of your swing and don't have as far to go. But you have to get them to make that turn. Let the inner circle control the outer circle, so to speak.

Let the inner circle control the outer circle.

I have some pictures of Sam Snead that were taken in 1947, and when he gets the club just past waist high, everything is finished except the arm swing. He already has the shoulders turned and the hips turned. He's in perfect position and all he has to do is finish swinging his arms to the top.

To my knowledge, there's not a player on Tour who thinks about his arm swing. They think about turn.

Ben Hogan, after he rebuilt his swing, had a relatively short arm swing but an enormous turn. Doug Sanders in his prime had what looked like a short swing because his arms didn't go back very far. But he had a very wide swing because he made a good turn, and he got plenty of distance. Dan Pohl looks like he takes the club only about halfway back. His arms stop swinging when his body stops turning. But he has a big turn, and he's one of the longest hitters on Tour.

A lot of the older players—Paul Runyan, George Fazio and Byron Nelson are good examples—tended to drag the club starting back. Basically, all they were doing was getting an early turn. The body was starting while the arms, hands and clubhead were left behind for an instant. But they always caught up. It's a pretty relaxed way to swing. You don't see this drag much anymore with the faster, more dynamic swings, but it might help a lot of amateurs play better.

So, while the ideal is starting everything back at the same time and the reality is probably that the arms start a fraction early, you should think about making your turn as early in the swing as possible. It's almost as if those bigger muscles need a head start. I like to think of turning my shoulders. In a good golf swing you need as big a shoulder turn as possible, you have some measure of hip turn, you have some movement of your feet and legs and you have an arm swing. And you need to put them all together.

No matter what your handicap is, I promise you'll play better if you do that. It's pretty simple—the more you can keep it together, the more you use every muscle in your body rather than being dependent on just one part, the farther and straighter you're going to hit the ball.

Footwork is extremely important and much overlooked. It's like dancing—there's a lot going on above the ankles, but the most important movements are with the feet. If you watch an old Fred Astaire movie, notice that whenever he is dancing you see the full length of him, because he wanted you to be able to observe his feet along with the rest of his body.

A lot of golfers are so concerned about their turns or their arm swings or their weight transfers that they fail to use their feet as effectively as they should. Every good player, no matter the width of his stance or what type of shot he is trying to play, has good footwork. Even in the smallest pitch shot, there is some movement of the feet.

The more you use every muscle in your body ... the farther and straighter you're going to hit the ball.

THE SWING

TURN BACK IN ONE PIECE

The backswing turn should start in one piece, preferably
generated by the shoulders, with the upper body, feet and
legs, arms, hands and club going back together. The weight
goes to the right side on the backswing. At the top (Frame 6),
the shoulders are fully turned and the hips are somewhat
restricted. The club, in this swing with a driver, is about

parallel to the ground, with the left arm reasonably straight but not rigid. The first move down (Frame 7) is with the lower body as the hips start to turn and clear. The head stays behind the ball as the right side fires through impact with the left leg straightening (Frame 10), and the weight goes fully to the left side, resulting in a straight-up position at the finish.

STRAIGHT BACK, THEN INSIDE

The club starts straight back but moves inside (Frame 2) as the body turns, especially with the driver. The turn gets the club behind you as the arms swing it up. The weight of the club forces the hands to start cocking instinctively (Frame 3). With the club behind you at the top (Frame 6), it can be

swung down from the inside and straight down the target line at impact (Frame 10), then back to the inside on the follow-through. At the finish the hands are relatively low, about ear-height, and the club has been swung more around the body.

FACE LEFT AT FINISH

This view of the driver swing from the target shows the club swinging to the inside as the body turns (Frame 2). At the top (Frame 4) the club is well behind the target line, ready to be swung down and straight through. The hips are clearing rapidly down and through impact (Frames 5 and 6), and at the finish the body is facing left of the target.

Swing barefooted to feel your footwork.

That's why it's so important to start in a balanced position, with the weight distributed between the balls and heels of the feet. As the swing starts, the weight should transfer toward the right side. But I want to caution you against lifting the left heel too much on the backswing. The weight can transfer without lifting the heel at all. If it needs to come up an inch, OK, but not more. Lifting the heel too much promotes a lifting, vertical swing without much power. Remember, never sacrifice balance, and it's hard to be in balance if you are "toe dancing."

On the forward swing, the opposite movement takes place. The weight goes strongly to the left side as you swing through impact. Try to keep the left foot from rolling to the outside as you swing into the follow-through. This keeps you in perfect balance. In the follow-through and at the finish you should have almost 100 percent of your weight on the left foot.

All of this happens at the same time the body is turning and the arms are swinging. Good footwork will help you make a better turn, both back and through. Some good players actually feel they push off with their feet in each direction. I practice good footwork all the time, even without a club in my hand, and you should too. Just move your feet in the way I've described, and you'll feel them turning your body even if you're not trying to. Sometimes it helps to swing barefooted to feel your footwork.

Your turn gets the club behind you, where it has to be at the top of the swing. Your arms swing the club up. Ideally, the club starts straight back, but it doesn't go straight back very long if you are turning your body. I don't like to see the arms break away from the body. I want them to maintain their position relative to the body early in the backswing. If the shaft at address points to your belly button, it should be pointing to your belly button at least a quarter to a third of the way into the swing. That means you made a nice early turn. At some point the arms are going to swing away and up, but by that time you have the good turn established.

A good way to find the perfect turn is to stand straight up, hold your arms out in front of you, cock the club up by your right ear and then just turn your shoulders fully. You're now turned with the club in the correct position, except that you don't have a posture that allows you to hit a ball on the ground. From that position you could make a swing and hit a baseball, as I'm sure many of you have done. Well, just put that swing on a tilt by bending at the hips and knees and you have a perfect golf swing.

I don't think about cocking my hands, or setting the angle, on the backswing. I believe that if you swing everything back together, centrifugal force and the weight of the clubhead will force you to cock your hands instinctively at the right time. I really disagree with attempting to set the angle early, for the reasons I've just talked about. If you're concentrating on setting the angle quickly, you'll tend to just pick the club up with your arms and not get any turn.

I see very few great players who set the angle early. Seve Ballesteros sets it earlier than most, but Seve has very long arms, is bent over quite a bit from the hips and carries his hands low at address. With this low hand position the angle is naturally set earlier and the swing is more vertical. But Seve also makes a very big turn, which is why he hits it so far. He's turning the club back with his shoulders while his hands and arms are swinging it up. Johnny Miller is another example. He is tall, with long arms, and his hands are low at address. So he cocks the club up pretty quickly, but he's making a good turn at the same time.

Hubert Green is another who sets the club early from about the same address position. He tends to do it so quickly that he has to be careful or he doesn't get enough turn. But, with two major championships and a bunch of other wins, he's been pretty successful with his method.

Those are exceptions, players with great athletic ability. If you just swing and turn everything back together, the angle will get set when and where it's supposed to.

The length of your backswing is determined by how supple

4-WOOD

LONGER CLUB, LONGER SWING

The longer the club, the longer the swing probably will be, as in this comparison of the 4-wood, 5-iron and pitching wedge. But that's a function of the length of the club, the width of the stance and the address posture. Note that with each club the shoulders are fully turned at the top of the backswing.

5-IRON

WEDGE

you are—how much your body can turn and how far you can swing your arms back. I suppose the ideal would be to have the clubshaft no more than parallel at the top. There are wonderful players who did and do swing past parallel, especially with the driver. Sam Snead did. Ballesteros did early in his career. Tom Watson does. But they are doing it with a good turn and are supple enough to go that far without anything breaking down. They also are strong enough to control the club. I think that most long swings, those that go past parallel, happen because the arms break away from the body turn. Generally speaking, if you have a good early turn there is not nearly the need for a long arm swing, because you already have so much power stored in your body turn. If you don't turn well, your arms must supply the power, so your swing will tend to get a little long.

I speak from experience. I've had a tendency to overswing, probably because my turn wasn't good enough and my arms were breaking away. But I've tried to correct that.

You're at the top of your backswing when you can't go back anymore.

You know you're at the top of *your* backswing when you can't go back anymore, when you can't turn your shoulders or hips anymore and you can't swing your arms back any farther without collapsing the left wrist or elbow. The club may or may not be parallel, but don't force it beyond where your body lets you go.

The left arm should be *reasonably* straight throughout the backswing. It definitely should not be rigid and can even bend a little at the top. That helps keep you more relaxed. And don't worry, centrifugal force will straighten the arm and maintain the axis of your swing through impact.

The *plane* of your swing is simply the angle of the arc of your clubhead as you swing back and through. That plane will tilt somewhere between vertical or straight up and down, which doesn't happen, or horizontal, which is back and forth along the ground. That doesn't happen either. Your plane is influenced by your physical characteristics and how you stand to the ball at address. If you are thick-bodied or have short arms, you probably will stand a little farther away from the ball, a little more erect with your arms extended, and you'll tend to swing a little more around yourself. That's a swing that's flatter or deeper. If you are thin and supple—or tall—you might tend to bend more from the hips, stand closer to the ball, set your hands lower at address and create a swing plane that is more vertical or upright. Or you may be somewhere in between.

In any event, if you set up to the ball in a position compatible with your build and make a good turn while you're swinging your arms, keeping everything together starting back, your plane will pretty much take care of itself and you won't have to worry about it.

Your plane also will vary depending on the club you have in your hand. That's because your posture changes. Your upper body is more tilted with the short irons, more erect with the driver. But the length of the club takes care of that.

The amount of your hip turn, and to some extent your shoulder turn, determines the type of shot you hit. Or maybe it's the other way around. Most of the guys with a fade-type swing, particularly those with strong grips, will have a very restricted hip turn on the backswing and will really turn or clear the hips coming through. This lets them swing the club straight down the target line. Paul Azinger and Lee Trevino are perfect examples. The players who draw the ball tend to have more hip and shoulder turn on the backswing and less clearing of the hips coming through. The farther you turn on the backswing, especially with the hips, the harder it is to clear, to get totally out of your own way. So your forward swing will come more from inside the target line and the ball will tend to draw.

So, depending on the kind of shot you want to hit, you must do something to increase or restrict your hip turn. If you want to turn the ball from right to left, you might want to close your stance by dropping your back foot farther back from the target line. That will allow a bigger hip turn. If you want a left-to-right shot, you could open your stance by dropping your front foot back from the line. That will help

Your plane will pretty much take care of itself and you won't have to worry about it.

restrict your hip turn.

I now try to restrict my hip turn some compared with my earlier days on Tour. I've always had the problem of swinging too much in to out, a result of that short, flat swing I grew up with. I still had that tendency even after I changed to a longer, more upright swing when I started working with Bob Toski. My swing would get too steep, and I'd get the club above the correct plane at the top. Then I'd drop it inside coming down, hang back with a lot of knee flex and finish with my body in a severe "reverse C" position.

Because of this in-to-out path, I had a tendency to hang the ball to the right—sometimes at the most inopportune moments. Or I had to recover with a lot of hand action. With the longer clubs the low point of my swing was too far behind the ball. By the time I got to the ball, the club had already started to come up and I was almost hitting it with topspin. That's fine with a driver, if you tee it high, but it doesn't work with the other clubs. My short iron shots flew too high and my long irons and fairway woods were too low. I couldn't hit a 3-wood off anything close to a marginal lie and make it carry well.

In 1982 at San Diego, the year Johnny Miller won, I came to the last hole needing a birdie to tie. It's a reachable par 5, but it has a pond in front of the green. I hit a good drive and certainly should have been able to reach the green in two with a 3-wood. But the ball was on a slight downslope and the lie was a little tight. For me to make the green from a lie like that with my swing was difficult if not impossible. But, needing the birdie, I felt I had to try the shot and hope for a miracle. I hit it in the water and made bogey, and that really hurt.

A few years later, after I'd improved my technique and was not hanging back on my right side, I had a similar lie on the hole and was able to knock a 4-wood onto the green with no problem.

One day I was telling Jim Ferree, who is one of the best ball-strikers around, that my swing was too in-to-out and I needed to change it. He said that almost every good player has gone through the same thing. As beginners, most players have some alignment problems, usually aimed way to the right. They don't have enough turn and just lift their arms. So they come over the top, chop down and hit a slice. So for the first part of their golf careers they try to get out of swinging over the top. They learn to do that by taking the club back pretty straight and dropping it inside on the downswing. Now they can hit the ball without a slice, learn to hook the ball and start to become better players.

But later they get to swinging in to out too much and are hitting the shot that every professional and good amateur fears, the hook. So they have to go back and learn what feels like the slice swing again. It isn't, because they're taking the club straight back and straight through, but it feels like it.

It's surprising how many amateurs, even higher handicappers, have the in-to-out problem. The common conception of a high handicapper is someone who comes over the top and either pulls the ball or hits a pull slice. But "over the top" has become, in golfers' minds, such a move to be avoided that they go too far the other way. I see a lot of amateurs who start the ball to the right, get a hook that makes the ball end up left of the target and think they've come over the top. How could they come over the top and swing the club to the left when the ball started right of target? They were too much in to out and had too much hand action.

For me to overcome this problem, I have to feel that the low point in my swing, with the fairway woods and irons, is on the target side of the ball, and to do this I do almost feel that I'm coming over the top. I'm really not, but that's the feeling I have.

By restricting the hip turn some, it makes my backswing a little flatter so I don't need to drop the club to the inside on the downswing. It's already inside. This allows me to have more of a free forward swing. As I start my forward swing I concentrate on clearing my hips, turning that left hip out of the way very, very fast. If I restrict my hip turn on the

Good players have to go back and learn what feels like the slice swing again.

4-WOOD

5-IRON

WEDGE

PLANE CHANGES WITH CLUB

The plane of the swing varies with the posture at address, which in turn is influenced by the length of the club. With the 4-wood, the upper body is more erect, so the plane of the swing is flatter or more around. As the club gets shorter, the body is bent more from the hips and the plane gets more upright. There is no need to think about this—the length of the club and the posture take care of it.

SWING REMAINS THE SAME

This three-quarter view of the driver and 5-iron swings show that the golf swing is basically the same no matter what club is in the player's hands. Again, the shoulders are fully turned at the top and the hips begin to clear immediately at the start of the forward swing with each club. Despite the differences in

stance width, length of club and aggressiveness of the swing,
the body positions are remarkably similar at the same stages.
There is no need to learn a different swing for each club.
One will do nicely.

Prior to Jack Nicklaus, very few players had an upright swing and finished in the reverse C position.

backswing, it helps me clear faster going forward. So I've widened my stance and set the right foot more square, which restricts the hip turn, and I've angled my left foot out more. Not only does this also help restrict the hip turn going back, it helps clear my hips faster on the downswing.

Once I get myself in a position where the left side is clearing, there is nothing to get in the way of the right side. It can just fire right on through, and now I know what Ben Hogan meant when he said he wished he had two right hands to hit with. Clearing my left hip faster allows me to stay more centered over the ball at impact, which allows the right arm to extend after impact and stay straighter longer. The right shoulder moves past where the ball was and the left arm begins to fold soon after impact. I can move right on into a follow-through with all my weight on the left side and the club going more around my body. At the finish my body is pretty straight up and down, with none of the old reverse C.

The cycles in the golf swing over the years are interesting to watch. Prior to Jack Nicklaus, very few players had an upright swing and finished in the reverse C position. Walter Hagen didn't do it, Bobby Jones didn't, Ben Hogan didn't, Sam Snead didn't, Arnold Palmer didn't. I guess you can go all the way back to Harry Vardon. Almost all the great players had swings that were flatter and more around their bodies. They finished in a straight-up position with the weight totally on the left side. The right arm began to fold at the moment of takeaway and they kept the right elbow tucked in close to the body on the backswing, which helps provide power. Then the left arm folded into the side on the follow-through. Instructors used to have their students tuck a handkerchief under the right arm and keep it there during the swing.

Then Nicklaus came along with a very steep, upright swing, his hands reaching for the sky and his right elbow flying out from his body. The experts said this kid couldn't make it because he had this flying right elbow. Little did they know that he had legs that were 30 inches in circumference, that he was going to make more putts than anybody ever and that he had one of the best minds in the history of the game. He tends to hang back, not getting fully onto the left side and finishing in a reverse C. But he's strong enough to get away with it. And look what he has done.

But suddenly almost everyone was swinging more upright and with the reverse C because the best player in the game was doing it. Gary Player, who patterned himself after Hogan, didn't. Neither did Lee Trevino, who was self-taught. But players my age who grew up watching golf on TV began to pattern their swings after Nicklaus. Tom Watson did. So did Ben Crenshaw, Curtis Strange and Tom Kite. Unfortunately, most golfers don't have the strength or talent of a Nicklaus.

Now we are getting into an era where a number of instructors are teaching flatter swings. They're seeing that the reverse C causes some golf problems as well as back problems, and a lot of their students are just not strong enough to be able to play with it.

I now feel that flatter is better. There is less strain on your back and more power going to the target because you are moving through toward your left side. And more and more good players are doing it. Watch Curtis Strange now. Peter Jacobsen is a prime example. Robert Gamez is an example of a fine young player who swings flatter, finishing more around with his weight fully on his left side. Orville Moody and Miller Barber are among many on the Senior Tour who finish that way. Even Nicklaus in recent years has tried to flatten his swing a little. He calls it "deeper," but flatter means the same thing.

Moving through the shot and getting your weight to your left side is critical to hitting good shots. But, like everything else, don't overdo it. My head moves a little toward the target in the through-swing, but it does so after impact, when the ball is already long gone. Throughout the backswing and through impact you want to keep your head as steady as possible. I prefer to think of keeping your spine angle con-

> Flatter is better. There is less strain on your back and more power going to the target.

It's a two-sided game. Both arms, both sides have their own jobs.

stant, not letting your spine move up and down or change positions very much. It can slide to the right slightly on the backswing. Curtis Strange is one who does this noticeably, more than I'd recommend for most players. But I'd much rather have it going that way than having a reverse weight shift. You have to get your weight to the right side before you can get it back to the left on the forward swing.

Assuming you were in good balance at address, maintaining your spine angle keeps you in good balance as you swing back and through. Again, don't overdo. Don't try to stay so rigid with your spine that you lose freedom of motion. You want to encourage motion. Develop a feel for a steady spine angle in practice so you can go out on the course and play and not have to think about it.

Which arm or hand do you control the swing with? That's just feel. It's a two-sided game. Both arms, both sides have their own jobs. If you have a tendency to overcontrol the swing with your right, then you probably need to think more about your left side for a while. If you tend to lead too strongly with the left side, then you should think a little more about your right.

I haven't said much about hands, and I won't. The hands are connected to the golf club, and that's about their only role. That's important enough and is the reason you should have a good grip. But think of the hands only as a connection. The rotation of the body and arms is what releases the club through impact. And that will happen as a reaction if you've done everything properly beforehand.

We hear and read a lot about a "late release" or the "delayed hit." We see pictures of professionals coming into the ball with the hands still cocked and the angle between the left arm and shaft still very acute. And it's true that the hands do release, but that's caused by the centrifugal force created by the turning of the body and the swinging of the arms. For most amateurs, trying to delay the release means they don't get the clubface square and consequently slice the ball. Then they start to make compensating moves that get their swings all whopperjawed.

The most efficient release returns the shaft pretty close to vertical at impact and the clubface to square, so a good thought for most players is simply to have the shaft more or less in line with the left arm as the ball is hit. Assuming nothing funny has been done with the hands, that will bring the clubface square when and where it needs to be.

Basically, if you just clear your hips starting down so the arms can swing through as you move to your left side, the correct things will happen.

How fast should you swing? That's a question only you can answer, but I can give you some guidelines.

First, golf is a distance game. Accuracy is critical, of course, but you have to hit the ball a certain distance. To play a golf course well, you have to hit the ball far enough to get where you want to go in the right number of strokes.

Strength plays a part in the ability to hit a golf ball a long way. The stronger player will hit it farther than the weaker player, assuming his technique is as good. The good thing about golf, though, is that it is not just a strength game. Weight lifting is mostly a strength game, although even here technique is important. But in golf you have many other factors—touch and feel, mental discipline, knowledge of course management—that help you perform well on the course and shoot a good score, which is what we're after. Given all that, strength is not the most important factor.

Speed is important. I swing the golf club *hard*. That may not be the best word, but that's the feel I have. Your feel may be different, but whatever it is, you want to swing the golf club as fast as you can and still maintain control. You don't want to fall down, you want to maintain your spine angle and you want an on-center hit. If you don't hit the ball solidly, you'll never get your maximum distance no matter how fast you swing. If you're not getting solid hits, work on your technique. But I have a real problem telling people to slow down and swing easy if they are only hitting it 145 yards. They need to increase their swing speed.

To play a golf course well, you have to hit the ball far enough to get where you want to go in the right number of strokes.

One guideline to your best swing speed is how fast you can move your body. The people in the Centinela Hospital Fitness Trailer on Tour tell us that your arms will always keep up with your body. Turn your body as fast as you can, through and past impact, and the arms will always react instinctively and be able to keep up. The problem is that in many cases the body doesn't keep up with the arms. The key is to be able to keep everything together.

Tom Watson swings very fast and he keeps everything together well. Lanny Wadkins swings very fast and keeps it together. If you asked me to swing as fast as those two guys, I couldn't time it very well. I have to find *my* maximum effective speed, and so do you.

An efficient machine always runs easier and faster than an inefficient machine. So the more efficient your golf swing becomes, the farther you will hit the ball. I've seen many high handicappers who have the strength to hit the ball a long way, but they don't because their swings are not efficient. Then they feel they have to swing even harder, and their swings become even more inefficient.

The trick to swinging the club fast is to swing it fast at the proper time. Would you believe that former President Gerald Ford swings the club almost as fast as Jack Nicklaus? But Nicklaus hits the ball a lot farther. President Ford already has used up all his energy and speed by releasing the club too early from the top instead of saving it for impact. The players who swing the fastest effectively have a gradual buildup of momentum and speed during the early part of the swing and through impact, and they fully use every muscle, every square inch of their bodies, to generate maximum distance.

I've always had a reputation as a short hitter, and at one time I probably was, compared with most players on Tour. But as I've made my swing more efficient, I've gained a great deal of distance. I still won't win any driving contests, but there aren't any holes I can't handle.

One problem with the thought of swinging hard and generating a lot of clubhead speed is that often, in the amateur

An efficient machine always runs easier and faster than an inefficient machine.

player, it induces tension. The muscles tighten in the effort to swing harder, and just the opposite happens—tight muscles inhibit speed.

Try this for yourself. Hold a pen or pencil as lightly as possible without having it slip out of your hand—not loose but light. Now write a sentence, legibly and as quickly as possible. Next squeeze the pen as tightly as you can and try to write the same sentence. See how much longer it takes.

The same thing happens in the golf swing. So the secret is to relax the muscles as much as possible while still keeping control of the club.

How tight is tight? That's a feel that you have to develop for yourself. It's like the fellow who was reading a putt, and he asked his old caddie if the putt broke as much as he thought it did. The caddie replied, "I don't know how much you think it does." What's a tight grip for one may be a light grip for someone else. The key is to allow your muscles to move freely and without excessive tension.

Tempo puts the swing together, allowing it to work efficiently and at its most effective speed. Tempo is the relative rate of movement of your body parts, the rhythm and timing of your swing. Your different parts work at different speeds at different times, and they must do that in the proper sequential motion. The speed of your swing from start to finish has little to do with it, *as long as that speed lets the parts work as they're supposed to.* Tom Watson has a much faster swing than Jack Nicklaus, but they both have great tempo. Both keep everything working in the right sequence during the swing and both hit great shots consistently.

When I'm playing really well, I'm thinking tempo. I have to think about tempo a lot, because my arms tend to break away from my body. I feel I have to slow my arm swing to give my body a chance to turn. Toski once told me that he didn't care which one I thought about. I could either think about slowing my arms, which allows me to turn, or I could think about turning, which slows down the arm swing. But either way, he said, they have to go back together.

Tempo puts the swing together, allowing it to work efficiently and at its most effective speed.

Golfers often blame poor tempo for bad shots when usually their mechanics are at fault.

That's what tempo does. It's really critical during the change of direction at the top. Most good players don't really stop at the top. Sure, the club stops, because it has to start going the other direction, but usually the hips start moving forward as the club is still moving back. There have been some good players who appear to pause at the top of the swing—Cary Middlecoff, Dan Sikes and Bob Murphy, to name a few. But that's just a function of their particular swing speed and tempo. No matter what the speed of your swing is, you always have to allow enough time to make the right sequential movements going back and coming down.

Nicklaus has said that when he wants to hit the ball farther he takes the club away more slowly. That's his way of making sure he allows enough time at the top to put all the parts in the right sequential motion so he can hit it harder coming down. But you can be *too* slow with the takeaway. I've always thought Hubert Green was too slow in the first couple of feet of his takeaway. From there on he gets very fast. He doesn't have a gradual buildup of speed. Several times a round you will see him getting too quick. I'm not being critical of Hubert. He has a great record, so the method works for him. But I'm sure he has to pay constant attention to his tempo.

Golfers often blame poor tempo for bad shots when usually their mechanics are at fault. Bad mechanics usually cause bad tempo, because you don't have the power stored up to be able to hit the ball the distance you need, so you instinctively try to make up for the lack of stored power by swinging too hard and too quickly from the top.

Let me remind you that everything I've discussed in this chapter is meant to be used as guidelines to build your own swing. We're not looking for pretty. We're looking for better golf scores. You might have a swing that's not too pretty, but if it works consistently and sends the ball where you want it, that's a lot better than having a nice-looking swing that is inconsistent.

Having a golf swing that works is only part of striking a

golf shot and playing golf. In the rest of this chapter I'm going to give you two keys to getting that swing started and making it work on the course to give you better scores.

How to visualize your shots. Before you step up to a shot, you need to visualize that shot. It's hard to go from Austin to Dallas if you don't know how to get there. You need a map or some directions. If you just jump in your car without a clue on how to get to Dallas, you might end up in Houston. But if you have a map, you have a pretty good chance of getting to your destination.

That's all visualization is—a map in your mind to help you get where you want to go. Visualization is a mental image of the type of shot you want to play and where you want the ball to end up.

Every good player, when he's playing well, has that map. He knows the road he wants to travel. Sometimes the road gets a little dark because he loses concentration and lacks focus on the shot he's trying to make. That's when the bad shots come.

Visualize your shots, not your swing. I try not to think about my swing while I'm playing, and I don't know of any good players who do. I'd recommend you don't, either. On the golf course you want to be playing, not thinking about your swing.

Many players talk about actually "seeing" the shot before they hit it. Jack Nicklaus talks about "going to the movies." Bruce Crampton once said he could see the ball flying through the air, landing on the green, bouncing and rolling toward the cup. Chip Beck says he has to see an "action track" of the ball curving or rolling into the hole.

Well, if you can see that action track or go to the movies, that's great. I've never been able to do that, but I still need a method of visualizing the shot. I first see where I want the ball to finish, the target. The lay of the land, the yardage to my target, the lie of the ball, the obstacles between me and the target dictate the club I choose and the type of shot I

That's all visualization is—a map in your mind to help you get where you want to go.

You always have to know how to get to Dallas before you start out.

want to play, be it high or low, be it right to left or left to right or dead straight. After making these decisions, I see where I want the ball to start and where I want it to end up. I sense and "see" the height I need and the shape of the shot. In effect, what is happening is that my mind is telling my muscles what it wants them to do.

A lot of that just comes from playing golf a long time and having a sixth sense for what the right shot is at a particular time. But it's something everyone should try to develop. Whatever method works best for you is the one to use. If you can see the action track, then look for it. Or sense the shot with your mind and muscles. Or use some combination of these methods. But do it on every shot. You always have to know how to get to Dallas before you start out.

How to establish your preshot routine. So you now have this wonderful map of the road to Dallas. But you're still sitting in Austin, and if you can't get the car started you aren't going to get there. The ignition, the key that allows you to start the car, is your routine.

Your routine is making sure the car is ready to go—you check the gas and oil, make sure your tires are inflated, get in the car, put on your seat belt, put the key in the ignition and turn the key.

Now the car is moving efficiently, just as your golf swing is moving. If you left out part of your routine—if you failed to check the oil level, for example—you may get halfway there, the engine will break down and the trip is over. It's the same in the golf swing. If you don't go through your routine correctly, your swing can break down.

The two things I try to think of most when I'm playing are *tempo* and *routine*. When I'm playing well, that's what I am thinking about. And the routine helps me set my tempo. Controlling the pace and number of my waggles and the number of times I look at the hole promotes a tempo that will help my swing work at its best.

Routine is just that, a matter of going through the same

motions every time as you prepare to start your swing. It's very important to be able to perform that routine consistently under pressure if you want your swing to perform efficiently. Dick Coop, a sports psychologist, says that your routine should trigger your concentration, that something in the routine should tell your body that this is now important and it had better start paying attention. Bert Yancey has said that the routine gets you through "the awful moment of take-away," and I guess to an extent he's right.

Your routine can be anything you want it to be. Maybe it includes a practice swing or two. I'm not sure I consider my practice swings part of my routine, but I know I can't play a shot without taking them. You set up to the ball a certain way, setting first one foot and then the other. Try to do it the same way every time. You take a certain number of waggles. You look at the target and back to the ball a certain number of times. You forward press and start your swing in a certain way. Keep it the same.

Your routine can be precise or it can be casual. That will probably depend on your personality. Jack Nicklaus has a very precise-looking routine. Lee Trevino just kind of steps up, moves his feet around a little, grips and re-grips the club and swings. But each of them does it the same way every time, at least when they make good shots. So be consistent with your routine to be consistent with your swing and your scores.

Yancey used to insist on going through his routine in precisely the same number of seconds each time. I don't see the time factor as that important. Yes, make it as consistent as possible, but doing it in 13½ seconds each time is not nearly as important as doing the routine well, so that when you take that club back you are ready to play.

Your routine needs to be consistent for a particular kind of shot, but it doesn't need to be the same for all kinds of shots. Mine isn't. I have a different routine for the full shots, for the different short shots around the green and for the bunker shots. Obviously you're going to have a different routine for

Your routine can be precise or it can be casual. That will probably depend on your personality.

I'd much rather have you thinking about your routine than having mechanical swing thoughts running through your head.

putting. All the routines may be somewhat the same, but there can be some differences. The important thing is that your routine be the same for each particular shot.

As a rule of thumb, I'd say the less time your preshot routine takes, the better. Don't hurry, but the more time you spend in the routine, the greater your chance of allowing extraneous thoughts and tension to creep in. Nicklaus spends a lot of time over the ball during his routine, but he probably has greater mental discipline than most of us.

Practice your routines on the practice tee, the practice bunker and the putting green. Practice until you get them grooved so you are comfortable with each routine and trust it on the course, so you don't have to think about each move you are making. I do often think about my routine when I'm playing, but I don't have to consciously plan each step. I've played rounds when I would count my waggles as a way of establishing my tempo. I'd much rather have you thinking about your routine than have mechanical swing thoughts running through your head or have you worried about the results of the shot.

If you are familiar with a player, it's very easy to see when he's letting the pressure of a situation affect him. Invariably he will get out of his routine. It may be an extra waggle or an extra look at the target, but that's enough to destroy the rhythm of his routine. And, invariably, he'll hit a bad shot.

Go through your complete routine every time before you take the club away. Don't try to bypass it. If something happens to break your concentration, or you don't feel quite right over the ball, don't try to force your swing. Step back and start over again. Billy Casper has a routine that starts when he takes the club out of the bag. If he's interrupted as he prepares to make the shot, he actually puts the club back in the bag, then takes it out and starts over. I don't have to put the club back in the bag, but if something bothers me, I'll step away and begin again.

You should, too. It's hard enough to play this game well without approaching a shot haphazardly.

CHAPTER 3/ PLAYING THE STROKESAVERS

There was a tremendous joy in finally winning ... it raised me to a different level.

It took some of the swing changes longer to kick in than I'd anticipated, at least as far as winning was concerned. I won overseas in 1974, but I didn't win in the United States until 1976, my fourth full year on Tour.

I climbed up the money list every year—26th place in 1974, 18th in 1975. In 1976 I became the leading money-winner on Tour among players who had *not* won. That may be a dubious distinction, but it's better than *not* being the leading money-winner without a victory.

Finally, in June of 1976, I won the IVB-Bicentennial Golf Classic in Philadelphia. I shot 66 in the final round for a 277 total and beat Terry Diehl in a playoff that went five holes.

That year I finished 21st on the money list. I haven't been out of the top 20 since.

There was a tremendous joy in finally winning a tournament and getting that little monkey off my back. It raised me to a different level.

There have been a number of people, including good friends, who have been amazed at my ability to play well and finish high while making major swing changes. You're not supposed to be able to do that out here. As Sam Snead is supposed to have said, "Ya dance with the girl that brung ya"—or something like that.

I'm sure I sacrificed some immediate gains by changing my swing. I might have played better the first few years if I had just gone with what I brought to the Tour. But my goals were long-range. I had to tell myself that no matter what it cost or how long it took, I was going to make those improvements. I could either have success right now to a limited extent or later to a much greater degree. I decided I'd rather have it greater later.

In the meantime, I was able to survive pretty nicely on Tour. That's because I've been lucky, in a sense. I go back to the story of Cindy Figg-Currier on the LPGA Tour. In her early years she developed such a good short game that she has the luxury of being able to make some swing changes and improve her long game over a period of time. I was the same way. I had such a great short game that even when I hit it poorly I was going to play pretty well and score well. I've never quite figured out a way to get it up and down from the ball washer, as somebody once said I could, but I could get it up and down from almost everywhere else. If I happened to hit it well at any given time, then I was going to play and score really well. It's still that way, in fact. So I was able to make the swing changes and improve my long game and never really go into a major slump. My game never really disappeared.

A good short game also helps me play the tough courses well. In the 1974 U.S. Open at Winged Foot, in just my second full year on Tour, I was striking the ball badly, which is not exactly what you want to be doing in an Open. But I kept making miraculous recoveries for four days and finished tied for eighth at 293, just six shots off Hale Irwin's winning total. It was only because of my short-game ability.

I remember something Mr. Penick once said to Ben Crenshaw and me: *"You don't practice your bunker game in an-*

I've never quite figured out a way to get it up and down from the ball washer ... but I could from almost everywhere else.

ticipation of your misses. You practice your bunker game so you can become more aggressive." In other words, if a flag is tucked behind a bunker or next to a bunker, you can fire at it without fear. If you miss, you know you can get it up and down from the bunker. It's the same for all shots around the green. Maybe that's why we always have been magicians at recovering from trouble.

The short game is the number one factor in playing and scoring well. If you can develop a good short game, then it's no problem experimenting with and trying to improve your full swing. I like to think that you improve your long game to lower your highest scores. But to lower the low scores you must improve your short game.

The first thing in building a short game is to establish your *order of preference,* what shot is best to play under the conditions. My preferences are to putt the ball with a putter where conditions allow it. If I can't do that, I will chip the ball with almost every club in the bag, increasing the loft as it's necessary. If I'm too far away to chip or don't have enough green to work with, I'll play some sort of pitch-and-run shot. If I can't do that, I'll go to a high lob or cut shot.

That's my personal order of preference. I was taught by Mr. Penick that the lower the shot, the easier it is to control under pressure situations. If you are pitching pennies at the wall or to a line, you get down low and pitch the coin low. You don't make a high, floppy pitch.

But your first consideration should be what shot you play best. If the conditions warrant, you should play that shot. The conditions you have to analyze include the lie of the ball, the length of the shot, how far you are off the green, how much green you have to work with, any slopes or elevations and the condition of the turf between you and your target. The relative safety of the shot also is a factor. But, whenever possible, play your best shot. You'll be more comfortable with it and have a better chance of getting the ball close to the hole.

In all cases, it's best to get the ball on the ground as quickly

'You practice your bunker game so you can become more aggressive.'

as you can and let it run to the hole. If you're going to control something, the lower you get it the better off you are.

THE OFF-GREEN PUTT

This is the "Texas Wedge" shot, so named because it could be played a lot on the hard fairways in Texas. It may not always be the best shot, but it's the safest shot from off the green because you eliminate the spin you have with lofted shots, and you eliminate any confusion about how far you have to carry the ball before it lands and starts rolling. It also works best when your nerves are jangling.

In putting from off the green, first consider the condition of the grass between you and the edge. If it's bumpy or thatchy or too long, you'd better go to a lofted club. Consider any slopes, of course. Finally, you have to determine how hard you want to hit the ball. There is no rule of thumb that determines how much harder the ball needs to be hit through fairway and fringe areas than if it were solely on the putting surface. That will vary with the length of the grass, the firmness of the turf and how much fairway and fringe need to be covered. You should practice the Texas Wedge shot to get a feel for it. Only through doing something can you learn it.

THE CHIP

In chipping, from good lies, I use a method popularized by Paul Runyan, one of the all-time short-game masters. Every chip shot is hit with a putting stroke. I use my putting grip, the reverse overlap. I use my putting stance, positioning the ball slightly forward of center and setting my weight slightly left to insure tapping down on the ball with a slightly descending blow. Mr. Penick calls it "hitting the crotch of the ball," the point where the ball and the ground meet. If the ball is sitting down in the grass, play it a little farther back in your stance and maybe set your weight a little more left. The grass is your enemy on chip shots, so the more you can do to avoid catching grass between your clubface and the ball, the better off you are.

THE CHIP WITH THE PUTTING GRIP

With this method, which I recommend, use the reverse overlap putting grip. If you have a good lie, set the ball slightly forward of center and your weight slightly left, then use your putting stroke, tapping down slightly on the ball and swinging through as if it were a putt.

THE CHIP WITH THE REGULAR GRIP

*When more distance, and therefore more clubhead speed, is
needed, try the regular full-shot grip, which allows more
hand action. But the arms and hands remain stable, with no
flippiness, returning at impact to approximately the same
position as at address.*

THE CHIPPING STROKE IS INSIDE TO INSIDE
The chip with the putting grip is a simple back-and-through motion, done with a combination of the arms, hands and shoulders. As in the putting stroke, the club starts straight back and moves slightly to the inside on the backswing, then back to the inside on the follow-through. Try to make this as much like your putting stroke as possible.

It's a better way to chip when you're under pressure. With fewer moving parts, there is less that can go wrong.

In all cases, the club will rest slightly on the toe, because the iron is designed to sit farther away from the ball for a normal shot. I use basically a one-lever system, swinging arms and shoulders without adding a whole lot of body or wrist action. Let the hands work naturally on the longer strokes, but don't consciously use them.

This method causes the ball to come out fairly dead, with very little backspin, so you can control the distance better. It lands softly and almost immediately starts to roll. You also can hit the chip shots a lot straighter because there is less sidespin. And it's a better way to chip when you're under pressure. With fewer moving parts, there is less that can go wrong.

I hole a lot of chips. One of the best came at the Bay Hill Classic in 1982 when I chipped in from the fringe on the first playoff hole, the 15th, to beat Jack Nicklaus and Denis Watson. I was three feet off the green in the short fringe, 18 feet to the left of the hole. I definitely was feeling the pressure at the time, but I'd been chipping well all week. I hadn't made any, but I'd lipped a couple out and had come so close on others that I felt I was due. I was definitely trying to make this one. The chip I hit was no different from the others. It just happened to go in.

I used an 8-iron for that shot, but I chip with a lot of different clubs, depending on how far you have to carry the ball and the position of the hole. Again, get the ball on the ground as quickly as possible. If the pin is close or the slope is downhill, or both, I might "putt my chip" with a sand wedge. If the pin is a long way away, I might even use my 3-iron.

If you haven't used the one-lever system before, it will feel much different from the conventional style, and the ball will react a lot differently. At first you'll probably find that you come up short. But the solid control you have over your chips should encourage you. Good touch, a feel for the shot, is vital in chipping, so you'll want to practice to develop this touch. Experiment with different clubs from different distances so you'll know how far each carries and rolls.

With the putting grip and the one-lever system you can't generate a lot of speed and power, not nearly as much as with the conventional grip. So there will come a point where you're so far away you can't get the ball to the hole with the club required. Don't force it. At that point, you begin to pitch the ball.

THE PITCH

The pitch shot basically involves a little longer arm swing and more use of the hands to supply the power. This two-lever method enables you to hit the ball farther without strain. Some think of it as just a miniature golf swing, and for the plain vanilla pitch it is. But for certain special shots you have to do some different things, and this method allows you to do that.

Pitch shots usually are made with more-lofted clubs, especially the pitching wedge and sand wedge. Several years ago I added a third wedge, a "finesse" wedge, to my bag. It is shorter than normal at 33½ inches and has 60 degrees of loft with less bounce than my sand wedge. My regular sand wedge is 35¼ inches long with 55 degrees of loft. I experimented with the third wedge for two reasons—I wanted a club I could hit 70 yards, about 25 yards shorter than my sand wedge, with a full swing; I also wanted a club that would make the partial shots easier and would help me with the difficult shots around the green that required me to get the ball high in the air.

I had a short game that I felt was as good as anybody's in the business, but when I put that 60-degree wedge in my bag in 1981, my short game improved dramatically. It was like night and day. I'd never finished higher than 11th on the money list, and the year before I was 20th. The year after I started using the club I was first, and I've only been out of the top 10 one time since.

The key to hitting any shot is to create acceleration through the ball, and this is especially true on pitch shots. Most good players can do this and have good control over

When I put that 60-degree wedge in my bag, my short game improved dramatically.

You don't score with the longer clubs ... the pitching clubs are your scoring clubs.

distance with the full swing, but they run into trouble with the "in-between" shots that require a less-than-full swing. I know that was the case with me. Anytime I got well inside 100 yards, say from 20 yards to 70 yards, I had a big adjustment to make with my regular sand wedge. The 60-degree wedge allows me to make more of a full swing on the partial shots, which allows me to accelerate the club more easily and gives me better distance control.

I think you'll find the same to be true, and I encourage you to experiment with a third wedge. Your specifications might be different from mine. You might want the normal length of a sand wedge or more or less loft, depending on how far you hit the ball. Or, if you now use your pitching wedge for the partial shots, you might want to try your sand wedge for the shorter ones. That's as good as adding another club.

If you do add a third wedge, you'll have to take a club out of your bag, of course. I took out my 2-iron and made my 3-, 4- and 5-irons stronger so that I have five degrees difference in loft between them instead of the usual four. This allowed me to add the wedge and still not have a large gap between my woods and irons. You might even want to take out your 2- and 3-irons and add a 6- or 7-wood.

The point is, you don't score with the longer clubs. You're just trying to get the ball on or near the green. The pitching clubs are your scoring clubs, so why not have one more to help you get the ball closer to the hole?

Most players have trouble with the partial shot because they don't create smooth acceleration. They swing back too far, then instinctively decelerate on the forward swing. Or they don't swing back far enough and instinctively jerk it coming forward, which causes much too long a follow-through. To overcome these problems, *try to make your follow-through as long as your backswing.* Swing through as far as your backswing goes back. You now are regulating the length of your shot by the length of your swing, insuring a smooth acceleration through the ball into the follow-through.

Another advantage to making your backswing and follow-through equal is that you can maintain a constant grip pressure instead of grabbing or letting go of the club. You'll make solid contact more consistently.

For most pitch shots, I don't recommend gripping down on the club. That's especially true if you're using the wedges, which are a little shorter anyway. Gripping down too much makes the club feel lighter and promotes getting too quick and shortening the swing too much. Instead, try to control your distance with the length of your swing.

Many things go into your decision on which type of pitch to play—elevation, the slope of the green, intervening hazards and the amount of green between the fringe and the hole all have to be considered. But the lie of the ball may influence your choice of club and shot selection more than anything else. Don't try to play a shot that the lie won't allow you to play.

The pitch and run. The normal pitch shot or pitch-and-run *is* simply a miniature golf swing. There are no special mechanics involved. Play the ball off the inside of your left heel with a slightly open stance, your shoulders and clubface square to the target. Simply swing the club straight back and through and control your distance with your arm swing. It's the simplest, safest kind of pitch, and I play it every time I can. It can be played with almost any club, from the 4-iron up through the finesse wedge, depending on how far from the green you are, the amount of green you have to work with and the slope involved. The ball will have some backspin, of course, but will tend to run farther than other types of pitch shots.

A lot of golfers try to stick with their favorite club for different shots, varying the swing to compensate. I think it's safer and easier to stick with the same swing and simply change clubs to fit the circumstances. Practice with various clubs and on slopes, up and down, to get a feel for what you can do with each.

The normal pitch shot or pitch-and-run is simply a miniature golf swing.

Mr. Penick
always taught
us to keep
everything as
simple as
possible.

The high pitch. This can be either a lob, which stops more quickly because of its trajectory, or a cut shot, which spins more and will check up sooner.

It's important on these shots to widen your stance a little, stand a little farther from the ball and flex your knees more. Feel you are "sitting lower" to the ball. This will create a swing that's more around your body or flatter, which helps you feel as if you are sliding the club underneath the ball. The technique for both the lob and the cut is basically the same. To insure that I'm set up properly for these shots, I go through a routine that may help you. To begin with, I approach the ball with exactly the same alignment as for the normal pitch. Then I open my clubface, pointing it right of the target. How much I open it depends on how high I need to get the ball and how fast I need to have it stop. Now I move my feet and body around to the left until the clubface is pointing to the target. I feel as if I'm doing a little dance around the ball. This sets me left or open the correct amount. Now I make my basic swing along a line parallel to my stance line. I'm taking the club more up and outside and swinging it down across the line, but it feels like my normal swing.

Mr. Penick always taught us to keep everything as simple as possible, and that's the simplest way I know to play the different shots. Don't make any funny manipulations. Establish and control the desired trajectory with your setup procedure and ball position, then swing as you would for the normal pitch.

For the high lob, play the ball off your left heel. The higher you need to get the ball, the more you want to open your clubface and your stance. You want to make a slightly descending blow, but very slightly. As I said, feel that you're sliding the club under the ball. *But make sure you have a good lie.* This shot will only work if there's enough grass under the ball.

If your lie is tight or if for some other reason you need to play a cut shot with more spin, just move the ball back in your stance and use the same technique. You'll now be making a much more descending blow, pinching the ball more and creating more backspin. The ball still will come out fairly high and will stop more quickly on the green because it has spin as well as altitude. You'll need to swing a little harder because, with more backspin, the ball won't go as far. A harder, faster swing also creates additional backspin if you really need to get the ball to stop in a hurry.

These shots, especially, require imagination and creativity. You have to be able to visualize, to "see" the shot you want to make that fits the situation. At the moment, Mark Calcavecchia is the best on Tour at the little flop shots around the green. He won the British Open in 1989 by pitching a shot into the hole during the final round. That may be lucky, but not as much as you might think with Mark. He has the imagination to play these shots, he has very soft hands and he plays a lot of games when he's out goofing around. He tries to see how high he can hit a 20-yard wedge, how low he can hit it, how much spin he can put on it. And he's not afraid to play those same shots during a round, when it counts.

You should do the same. You have to imagine and practice these shots before using them on the course.

The low spinner. If you have a situation where you need to hit a sand wedge and the ball is in a bad lie, if you need to keep the ball low under a branch and stop it quickly or something similar, the low spinner comes in handy. If the pin is on the top of a ridge and your lie doesn't allow a normal pitch-and-run shot, you might want to land the ball just short of the ridge and make it skip up and check to a quick stop.

Just set up with an open stance and play the ball well back. This will put your hands ahead of the ball at address and encourage you to chop down with a sharply descending blow. The ball will come out low with a lot of backspin.

Lee Trevino plays this shot better than anyone I've ever seen. It's always fun to hear the gallery yell "bite" when he

> You have to be able to visualize, to 'see' the shot you want to make that fits the situation.

NORMAL PITCH

LOW PITCH

HIGH PITCH

PITCHING TECHNIQUES VARY

The techniques for the various pitch shots vary with the situation. The normal pitch or pitch-and-run is simply a miniature golf swing. Control the distance and the acceleration by making your backswing and follow-through the same length. For the low spinner, play the ball back in your stance and swing down with a sharply descending blow. For the high pitch, play the ball off your left heel, "sit down" to the ball with an open stance and feel you are sliding the clubface under the ball.

THE LOB SHOT

The lob version of the high pitch is done by playing the ball off the left heel, setting the stance open and swinging along the stance line. The ball will come out high and land softly with little spin. There must be enough grass underneath the ball to insure that this shot can be played safely.

THE CUT SHOT

The cut shot version of the high pitch is played when the lie is tighter or when you need to put some spin on the ball but still get it high. Play the ball in the center of your stance and use the same technique as for the lob shot, swinging along your stance line. A slightly descending blow will pinch the ball against the clubface and create more backspin.

hits it. They think that no shot that low could have any spin. Then it stops dead next to the hole. I'm sure that growing up on the Texas muni courses helped Lee become a master at the shot.

The pitch from rough. At the Georgia-Pacific Atlanta Classic in 1984 I had the lead going to the final hole of the third round. The 18th at Atlanta Country Club is a par 5 with water in front, reachable in two. I got over the water with my second shot but pulled it a little into the rough left of the green. Now I faced a shot that I had to carry over a bunker and land softly near the pin. Just on the other side of the hole was a ridge, and if I carried the ball too far it would catch the ridge and go forever. I'd have a 40-foot putt coming back.

Don Pooley was chasing me and was playing behind me. I wanted to have the lead going into the fourth round and figured I had to have a birdie to do that. I played a wonderful little pitch over the bunker that settled softly and ended up inches away from the hole. That gave me a 66 for the round and a one-stroke lead over Pooley. The next day I shot 67 and won by five strokes.

The technique for that shot is much the same as for the high pitch, except that it's played more like a sand shot. You set up to the ball as I described above, sit lower and feel you're sliding the club underneath the ball. Only in this situation you really do. Instead of striking the ball directly, you take a swath of grass out from under the ball. That swath should be a foot long or more, depending on the texture of the grass and how high or low the ball is sitting in it. This is an unpredictable shot, and it's tricky to gauge how far the ball will carry and roll.

Because the grass is cushioning the blow on the ball, you'll have to make a longer swing than normal to get the ball the proper distance. But be careful. You don't want to decelerate the club coming through the heavy grass, but you also don't want so much acceleration that the ball comes out hot and rolls too far. You're not going to get much backspin on

Instead of striking the ball directly, you take a swath of grass out from underneath the ball.

it, so you want it coming out high and soft. To do this, feel as if it's a dead-hands swing—somewhat of a one-lever action like the chip. The hands naturally will work a little, but you want to feel that the swing is primarily with the arms. Just swing back and down and let the momentum of the swing bring the club through the grass, clipping the grass from underneath the ball. Again, make your backswing and follow-through about the same length.

The pitch from a downhill lie. If you're on a downhill slope around the green, you should first consider putting the ball if the turf is smooth enough, or you might want to play a little pitch-and-run. Those are the safest shots. But sometimes you have to play a soft lob—if you have to pitch over a bunker, for example.

In that case, set your body as much in line with the slope as much as you can—your left shoulder will be lower than normal. Position the ball back toward the right foot. This combination of setup and ball position enables you to hit the ball with a descending blow and make solid contact. When you swing down, try to follow the slope with the clubhead for as long as possible.

The pitch from a severe upslope. When your ball is on the grass face of a bunker or other steep slope, you must set yourself in a stable stance. You have to make solid contact, so the one thing you want to avoid is moving on the shot. I set virtually all my weight on my right foot, my body tilted along the line of the slope, while my left side acts as a brace for me to hit against.

Then all you want to do is make a good, sharp blow against the ball, concentrating on keeping your left wrist firm at impact. Realize that the slope, in effect, adds loft to the club, so guard against popping the ball up and leaving it short. If you have a decent lie and enough green to work with, you might want to try an 8- or 9-iron. The ball also has a tendency to go left off these lies, because the heel of the club tends to dig in first before impact, so try to keep your club moving toward the target as long as possible.

Anytime the ball is on a steep slope, you have to make sure it doesn't roll after you've addressed it. If there is any doubt in your mind, don't ground the club. That way you avoid the penalty stroke if it does move.

THE SPECIAL SHORT SHOTS

There will come a time, maybe several times, in any round when you face a shot that requires unusual action. Here's where imagination and creativity play such a big part in golf. You have to consider the conditions and your ability and experience before deciding what type of shot to play. In most cases, play the safest shot first. When the conditions won't let you do that, or when a gamble seems justified, play the next safest shot.

I'll discuss three of the most common special shots and give you guidelines. You should try to figure out the best way for you to play them.

The shot from hardpan. Golf courses, even in the United States where the courses are often heavily watered, are especially susceptible to developing areas of hardpan around the greens, where people walk a lot, and particularly around the edges of cart paths near the greens. When your ball winds up in an area like this, your first choice should be the least-lofted club possible, starting with the putter, if the terrain allows you to run the ball to the green and the hole. If it doesn't, go to a more-lofted club. But be careful. The flange on a sand wedge will cause the club to bounce off the dirt and can result in a bladed shot that will sail over the green. If you have to pitch the ball over a hill or a bunker, a pitching wedge or 9-iron might be a better choice.

In any case, the shot calls for precise contact. Play from a slightly open stance and position the ball slightly back in your stance. This puts your hands ahead of the ball at address and helps to insure clean contact. Grip down slightly on the club

In most cases, play the safest shot first.

THE PITCH FROM ROUGH

Use a similar technique as for a high pitch, but play it like a sand shot, because you cannot contact the ball first. Sit lower with your stance and actually slide the club underneath the ball. Instead of striking the ball directly, take a swath of grass out from under it. You'll have to make a longer swing than normal to get the proper distance, because you are moving grass along with ball, and the grass deadens the impact. The swing is primarily with the arms, with very little hand action.

for better control and swing with confidence, crisply trapping the ball between the clubface and the dirt. The shot is really not as hard as it appears to be as long as you contact the ball first.

The bump-and-run up a bank. When your ball is well below the green surface, you're facing a bank and the hole is cut close to your side of the green, you have some obvious problems. If the circumstances of your match are such that you have to try to get the ball close, you can play the bump-and-run shot, provided the grass is not too heavy. Simply take a less-lofted club—a 5-, 6- or 7-iron—and make your normal pitching swing, driving the ball into the bank and letting it skip up onto the green. You have to develop a feel for the shot to know how hard to hit it. It's a shot that works if the grass if fairly short and the turf is firm. If the grass is too long, you risk getting the ball hung up in it. Or if the bank is too steep, the ball may not bounce up. Then you face another tricky shot. In that event, take your medicine and pitch the ball to the fat part of the green. Don't turn a one-shot mistake into a two- or three-stroke error.

The bellied wedge . . . and alternatives. If your ball winds up resting against the collar of rough that guards the green, you usually will have trouble making solid contact with a putter. The solution is the bellied-wedge shot.

Using your putting grip and stance, address the middle of the ball with the leading edge of your sand wedge. Then, with a putting stroke, try to hit the ball right in the equator. The shot is used a lot on Tour, although it's one I didn't learn until my fifth or sixth year out. It requires practice and a good touch, so don't try it if you haven't worked on it.

A couple of safer alternatives:

Before I learned the bellied wedge, I used to play this shot with a putter. Position the ball off your right foot, set your weight on your left side with your hands ahead of the ball. Cock the club up quickly and strike down into the back of the

Don't turn a one-shot mistake into a two- or three-stroke error.

THE PITCH FROM HARDPAN

*If the ball is on hardpan, use the least-lofted club possible,
starting with a putter. If you must pitch the ball, play from a
slightly open stance and position the ball back in your stance
to make sure you make precise contact.*

THE BUMP-AND-RUN UP A BANK

If the grass is fairly short and the turf is firm, you can run the
ball up a bank by taking a less-lofted club—a 5-, 6- or 7-iron
—and making your normal pitching swing. Drive the ball
into the bank and let it skip up onto the green.

THE BELLIED WEDGE

If your ball is resting against the collar of rough around the green, the bellied wedge shot often is an effective play. With your sand wedge, use your putting grip and stroke and strike the equator of the ball with the leading edge of the club.

THE BOUNCE OF THE SAND WEDGE

The bounce or flange or sole is the bottom of the club, the part that hangs below the leading edge. This part should hit the sand first so the club slides through the sand. The width of the flange and the amount it hangs below the leading edge should vary with the type of sand you usually play from. The wider the flange and the more it hangs down, the less the club will dig in the sand.

ball, causing it to bounce across the fringe and begin rolling to the hole. The steep, descending blow will help eliminate grass getting caught between the ball and club. Choose this shot if the hole is cut fairly close to you.

For a longer shot, or if the fringe is unusually rough, play the same shot with a 6-, 7- or 8-iron. The ball will carry the fringe and start rolling smoothly.

THE SAND SHOTS

Many amateurs are terrified when they get in the sand because of their past experiences. They've never been able to get the ball out consistently. They either blade it or leave it in the sand. The problem is simple. The most common error among amateurs in the bunker is that they don't use the bounce on the sand wedge because they don't get the clubface open enough. So the club gets stuck in the sand, which usually means the ball gets stuck there, too. So now they swing harder and faster and the club only gets stuck worse. Next they try to hit closer to the ball and take less sand to make sure it gets out, and eventually they'll blade the shot over the green. Now they really don't want to open the clubface because they think that's what caused them to blade the ball, when it really was just trying to hit too close to it.

The solution is just as simple. Swinging harder is not the answer. Using the bounce of the club properly is.

The bounce or flange or sole is the bottom part of the club that hangs down below the leading edge. You want that part to hit the sand first so the club slides through the sand. It's when the leading edge enters the sand first that the club gets stuck.

Generally, if you play mostly in soft sand, you want a club with a lot of bounce, a wide sole that hangs quite a bit below the leading edge. If you play in firm or hard-packed sand, you don't want as much bounce, because the sand itself insures that the club will bounce. A qualified professional can help you find a sand club that's properly designed for you and your course.

> Swinging harder is not the answer. Using the bounce of the club properly is.

They try to get open, but they're scared to open their shoulders, so all they do is open their feet.

The normal sand shot. I was taught the simplest possible way to set up to a bunker shot and insure that the leading edge doesn't dig into the sand. It's similar to the method I described for the high pitch shots. First address the ball with everything straight on—square stance, square body, square clubface. Then just open the clubface. That raises the leading edge and turns the back of the club down so the flange will hit the sand first. But now the clubface is pointing way right of the target. So you have to move your body around the ball until it is aligned left and the clubface is pointing to the target. Be sure to keep the clubface in the same relationship to your body.

Don't just drop your left foot back. That only opens your feet, not your body. That's where most people mess up in their bunker play. They try to get open, but they're scared to open their shoulders, so all they do is open their feet. You have to move around so your whole body sets up left.

Distribute your weight about 50-50 left and right for the normal sand shot. Then swing the club along your body line, just as for a high pitch. It's basically a normal swing, and you should just try to clip the sand out from under the ball, hitting three to four inches behind the ball. You can cock the club up a little bit more with your hands, creating a slightly steeper swing to insure that the bounce enters the sand first. But the address position you've established almost insures that most of those things will happen.

Chi Chi Rodriguez, who I think is the best bunker player around today, plays his shots exactly the way I do, except that he accentuates the action. He sets up very open and accentuates swinging his arms to the left, dragging the club through to make sure the clubface stays open and the bounce hits the sand first.

There are some variations among great bunker players. Gary Player is one of the best there's ever been. He has a squarer setup with his shoulders and he plays the ball back farther than most, picking the club up abruptly with his hands to the outside and coming in closer to the ball than any

THE SAND SHOT SETUP

To set up correctly for the normal bunker shot, first stand squarely to the ball with the club face square (1). Then open the clubface the desired amount (2). Next move your body around the ball, keeping the clubface in the same relationship, until your body is aligned left and the clubface is pointing at the target. Don't just drop your left foot back. Move your entire body until it sets left.

125

THE NORMAL SAND SHOT

Once you have assumed the correct address position, distribute your weight 50-50 and swing along your stance line. Strike the sand three to four inches behind the ball and try to clip the sand out from underneath it. You can cock the club up a little more with your hands, creating a steeper swing to make sure the club gets underneath the ball. Your open address position helps make this happen.

I'd rather you just swing the golf club the simplest way.

great bunker player I know of. He can do this because he's practiced his bunker shots by the hours and hours and that's how he does it best. It's a very risky shot, but if played properly it puts a lot of spin on the ball.

Phil Rodgers, another fine bunker player and instructor, doesn't want the swing going to the left. He wants you to use the bounce of the club by laying the club back and making sure you don't get your hands in front of the ball at impact. If anything, he wants you to get them behind the clubhead as you kind of flip it, using a steeper V-shaped swing.

You can play around with these methods if you want. But I'd rather you just swing the golf club the simplest way.

Higher handicappers who live in terror of bunkers probably get tired of hearing this, but the sand shot is one of the easiest in golf. There is more margin for error, because you don't have to hit the ball. All you have to do is aim at a point three or four inches behind the ball and cut a swath through the sand under the ball. Just take a shallow layer of sand out of the bunker and the ball will go with it. Feel as if you're spanking the sand behind the ball. It's like spanking a table with the back of your hand. That's the same type of bouncing action you need in the sand.

The distance your club enters the sand behind the ball will vary with the texture of the sand and your skill level. You determine that by practice. But don't get too close to the ball. You're better off hitting five inches behind the ball with a shallow cut than one inch with a deeper one.

You determine the distance your shots travel out of the sand by varying the length and speed of your swing. For a very short shot you take a shorter swing. If you have a long way to the hole, you'll take a longer and faster swing. Just react to the situation. Always keep in mind that because you're hitting the sand and not the ball, the bunker shot won't go as far as the normal pitch with the same amount of swing speed. You are moving a lot more weight with the sand than just 1.62 ounces of ball.

One of the most misinterpreted pieces of advice ever given—and you hear it a lot—is "don't quit on the shot" in the bunker. That immediately causes players to shorten the backswing and accelerate the club, and uncontrolled acceleration is what gets most golfers in trouble in the first place. Except for really long shots, the best bunker players I see don't have very long follow-throughs. I'd much rather see a long backswing with maybe even a little deceleration than a short backswing and a lot of acceleration coming through. If you use the bounce of the club properly to insure that the club doesn't dig, you don't need as much acceleration. You only need a lot of acceleration if you are going to extract a lot of sand by digging the sand wedge behind the ball.

For normal shots, take the club up to the top and feel that you are letting it fall, spanking the sand behind the ball. This will make the ball come out very softly and stop quickly.

The shot from firm sand. If you come across sand that is exceptionally firm or wet, you have to make a couple of adjustments. Here you do want to dig into the sand just a little. The firmness of the sand will insure that the club slides through under the ball, so there is no need to use the bounce of the club as much. I use my pitching wedge or my 60-degree wedge from hard sand, because they don't have as much bounce as my regular sand wedge, and it will pay you to experiment with that, too.

You could even go to a 9-iron or 8-iron. There's no law that says you have to use your sand wedge just because you're in the sand.

The high sand shot. Often you face a bunker shot where you have to pop the ball over a high lip and stop it quickly. The best and simplest way to get the ball high is to add loft to the club. Go through the routine I described for the normal bunker shot only open the clubface more. You also want to get wider with your stance and sit lower, as for the high pitch, so you feel as if you can really slide the club under the ball with a lot of loft still on the clubface.

Take the club up to the top and feel that you are letting it fall, spanking the sand behind the ball.

Just stick the club in there and leave it there.

Paul Azinger, who has led the Tour in sand saves a couple of times, really opens his clubface and stance when he has to get the ball up fast. He lays the club so open that you're sure he'll blade the shot. But he sits very low with a lot of flex in his knees, which insures that even with the extremely open clubface the club will slide underneath the ball and take out a shallow cut of sand.

The plugged lie. The thing you have to do with any bunker shot is clip the sand from under the ball. If the ball is plugged in the sand, really sitting down in it, then you obviously have to get the club deeper into the sand. To do that you have to make a steeper swing, one that is more abruptly up and down.

Given that, there are a couple of alternatives. One is to square or even close the clubface, which insures that the leading edge will dig in. If it digs in, you've got a real good shot at getting underneath the ball. The problem is that now you've taken loft off the club and the ball will come out low and running. Sometimes you have enough green to work with so you can do that, but not usually.

A softer shot is to keep the blade slightly open, cock the club up quickly on your backswing with your hands and, with a steep descending blow, just stick the club in the sand right behind the ball. There is no follow-through. Just stick the club in there and leave it there. Because you've done this with an open clubface and haven't taken off a lot of loft, you have a better chance of the ball coming out higher and softer.

The fried egg. When the ball buries in softer sand you're likely to end up with a fried-egg lie, the ball sitting down in a crater. The shot is played exactly the same as the plugged lie, with a steep swing and a sharply descending blow. Because you must hit so far behind the ball and extract so much sand, you have no choice—you have to square or close the clubface so the club will cut deeply enough through the crater to get underneath the ball.

THE FRIED EGG

From a fried-egg lie, when the ball is sitting down in a crater in softer sand, you must square or close the clubface. Make a steeper swing than normal, cocking the club up quickly with your hands and making a sharply descending blow into the sand to get the club underneath the ball. Strike the sand three or four inches behind the ball and make an abbreviated follow-through.

131

4

THE PLUGGED LIE

When your ball is plugged in the sand (below), you must make
a steep, up-and-down swing to get the club through the sand
and underneath the ball. You can square the clubface to do
this, which will give you a low, running shot, or you can
open it slightly to produce a higher, softer shot. With a sharp,
descending blow, just stick the club in the sand behind the
ball and leave it there. There is no need for a follow-through.

The ball will come out low and hot, so pay attention to what is past the hole.

The shots from slopes. A lot of bunkers have slopes, and unfortunately we all end up on them at one time or another. Then you have to make some adjustments.

I was taught a little trick to help me handle these slopes, and maybe it will clear up the problem for you.

Picture a board, maybe a 2x4, lying on the slope and you are standing above it, ball in hand. The object is to throw the ball onto the board in such a manner that it will bounce out of the bunker toward the hole. If you are on an *upslope,* throwing the ball steeply onto the board would deflect the ball backward. You must get low and throw a shallow pitch at the board so it will bounce out. On a *downslope,* a shallow pitch would cause the ball to bounce low and stay in the bunker, while a steeper throw would cause it to bounce out.

This is what you must do to play these shots. On the upslope, set your body with your weight on the right side and tilt your spine backward so you can take a shallow cut out of the sand. A steep or deep swing will just cause the ball to pop up, while the shallow swing will achieve some distance.

On the downslope, you *will* need the steeper swing to get the ball out. Set your weight left with your left side low. This sets your shoulders more parallel to the slope and makes it easier to make the steeper swing and get under the ball.

The same picture works for the side slopes. If the slope (and the 2x4) is tilted to the left, you must throw the ball more to the right to allow it to ricochet left toward the hole. The opposite is true with a slope to the right.

So if the ball is above your feet, align yourself to the right, knowing it will come out somewhat to the left. If the ball is below your feet, align your body left, because the ball will come out more to the right.

You also can combat these side slopes by either not digging in your feet or digging them in deeper depending on whether the ball is above or below your feet. If the ball is above, try standing on your toes to raise your body so it is more even with the ball. If the ball is below you, dig your feet in really deep to help get down to it.

The extra-long sand shot. The longer the sand shot, the more you want to make a longer swing with a shallower arc, which will send the ball out lower and farther. Occasionally you will face a shot that is simply too long for your normal sand wedge—30, 40, 50 yards or longer out of a bunker with a lip so high that you can't chip out of it. In that case, don't force it by trying to strike the sand closer to the ball. You can still control the distance by the length and speed of your swing by simply going to a less lofted club.

The extra-long explosion shot can be played with a lot of clubs. Go to a pitching wedge, then a 9-iron and so forth. Go as far down as a 5-iron. Use exactly the same procedure for the normal bunker setup. Open the clubface, set yourself left so the club is pointing at the target and make your normal swing, cutting into the sand three or four inches or so behind the ball. The longer clubs have less bounce, but if you open them and swing left along your body line, they still will slide through the sand. All of a sudden you have a longer range for your bunker shots without changing your technique.

Don't try to get fancy. If you're in the sand that far from the pin, getting down in two is not the issue. You don't want to hit the shot fat or skull it and take a bundle. You want to get the ball somewhere on the green, take your two putts and go on. If you happen to get it close enough for a one-putt—and you will occasionally—say thank you and smile.

It goes without saying, but I'm going to say it anyway—you must practice the extra-long shot to find out how far you can hit the various clubs. Without a lot of work here, this is no shot to try.

Practice all the shots I've described in this chapter. If you have a limited amount of time for practice, work on these first, before the full shots. You'll wind up saving strokes and smiling a lot.

See following photos.

> If you're in the sand that far from the pin, getting down in two is not the issue.

THE UPHILL AND DOWNHILL SAND SHOTS

If your ball is lying on an upslope in the sand (above), set your weight more on your right side and tilt your spine to the right, keeping your shoulders as close to parallel with the slope as you can. This will allow you to take a shallow cut out of the sand and get some distance with the shot. A steep swing

into the sand will just pop the ball up or drive it deeper into the sand. On a downslope (below), set your weight on the left, your left side low and your shoulders again more or less parallel with the slope. This will result in a steeper swing that lets you get the club underneath the ball, giving you the height that gets the ball out of the bunker.

THE SAND SHOTS FROM SIDE SLOPES

If the slope is toward you and the ball is above your feet (above), aim and align your body more to the right, because the ball will tend to come out to the left. Set your body a little taller so it is more even with the ball. If the slope is away from

4

*you and the ball is below your feet (below), align your body
to the left, because the ball will come out to the right. Dig
your feet in deeper and flex your knees more so you can get
down to the ball.*

3

4

THE HIGH SAND SHOT

To get the ball up over a high lip and stop it quickly, open the clubface more, widen your stance and flex your knees more to sit lower. Feel as if you are sliding the clubface under the ball.

141

THE EXTRA-LONG SAND SHOT

When you must make a shot out of sand that is too long for your normal sand wedge—and the conditions are such that you can't chip or pick the ball out of the bunker—simply go to a longer club. Use a pitching wedge, 9-iron, on down as far as a 5-iron, and use the same procedure as for a normal bunker shot. Open the clubface to get as much bounce on the club a possible, set yourself left so the clubface is pointing at the target and swing along your stance line, striking the sand three or four inches behind the ball. The longer the club, the less bounce it has, but with this procedure it should slide through the sand underneath the ball and greatly increase your range.

CHAPTER 4/ ROLLING THE BALL

The USGA rewarded me for doing what I was supposed to do.

The wins still weren't coming easily back in the '70s. After I broke through with my playoff victory at Philadelphia, it took me two years to do it again.

I had a couple of good chances, one coming in late August of 1978 at the Colgate Hall of Fame Classic in Pinehurst. I was tied for the lead in the final round when I addressed a short putt on the fifth hole. As I set my putter behind the ball, the ball moved. I think I was the only one who saw it, but I immediately called a penalty stroke on myself. As it turned out, that cost me a chance at a playoff. Tom Watson won the tournament at 277, and I finished in a three-way tie with Hale Irwin and Howard Twitty at 278.

Later that year I was given the Bob Jones Award for sportsmanship by the United States Golf Association. It's a prestigious award, and it was nice to be recognized. I got a lot of favorable publicity from it, but I had just done what was expected. The USGA rewarded me for doing what I was supposed to do. Players call penalties on themselves every month, maybe every week, on Tour. Playing golf within the rules is expected, whether it's for $50,000 or a $2 nassau or just for fun.

The next week, at the B.C. Open in Endicott, New York, I shot 267, 17 under par, and won by five strokes over Mark Hayes. Some said it was poetic justice. I'm not sure about that, but I can assure the second Tour win was very welcome.

Don't get me wrong. I hadn't been starving in the meantime. I had finished 14th on the money list in 1977, and the B.C. Open victory pushed me to 11th in 1978.

My ball striking was improving, but my short game was still carrying me. So was my putting, which is the final extension of the short game.

I have always—well, almost always—been able to make the ball roll true on the green, which is the basic thing in putting. Every good putter has that ability. If you don't get a true roll, you're not going to make a lot of putts. If you do, the ball almost seems to seek the hole.

The putt I hit on the final hole at Doral in 1984 was one of those. Going to the 18th I had a one-stroke lead over Jack Nicklaus, who was two holes behind me. My drive went a little into the right rough and I played a good 4-iron onto the green about 25 feet past the pin. Knowing Jack, he certainly was capable of making birdie on one of the last two holes to tie me if I didn't make the putt. I just poured the ball right into the hole, and all of a sudden the tournament was history. That putt had a true roll on it!

There's an excellent way of telling if you're getting a good roll. I learned this trick from Carl Welty, the teaching pro at LaCosta. Have somebody shoot some of your putts with a video camera. Take a striped range ball and place it on the green with the stripe perpendicular to your target line, then hit 20-foot putts. When you review the tape in slow motion, you'll be able to see how quickly the ball starts rolling. Generally it should skid for a short distance, a foot or less depending on the velocity of the putt, and then the stripe will start turning over. The quicker you can get the ball rolling and that stripe turning over, the better off you are.

If you don't get a true roll, you're not going to make a lot of putts.

The one thing you don't want to see is that stripe backing up before the ball starts rolling. That means you've hit it with too much loft on your putter, creating backspin and making the ball bounce. This will affect both accuracy and distance. The ball won't go as far when hit with the same force.

You have to hit the ball with a flat clubface. Negative loft can drive the ball down into the ground, and that will make it bounce. If you're on a firm, fast green, you may be able to hit the putt with a slight negative loft and actually get the ball rolling well. (You don't want to hit down on it, a point I'll discuss further when we get into the stroke itself.) But if you're on a thatchy green, like thick Bermuda, and you drive the ball the slightest bit into the ground, it will bounce, so you don't want negative loft there. In this case you actually need a slight bit of loft to help get the ball up on top of the thick grass so it can roll.

To get a true roll it's also important to hit the ball solidly. I'm convinced that more putts are missed because they are mis-hit than for any other reason. Sometimes I'll hit a drive 270 yards. A couple of holes later, under the same conditions, I'll hit one 250 with the same effort. The difference is that one was caught solidly and the other wasn't. It's the same with a putt. You won't see 20 yards difference, but you may see an inch or two or maybe even a yard or two on the longer putts. Even if you have read and aimed the putt correctly and get the blade swinging on the right path, the ball won't go the required distance and won't hold its line if it's not hit solidly.

I have never seen a person, if he has played a little bit of golf and has a little bit of ability, leave a long putt 10 or 12 feet short if he hits it solidly. I've never seen anybody who doesn't hit a makable 15-foot putt about the proper distance if he hits it solidly.

To make solid contact, you want to hit the center of the ball with the center of the club, measuring from top to bottom. And you want to make contact consistently at the same spot on the clubface, measuring from toe to heel. Ideally that

I'm convinced that more putts are missed because they are mis-hit than for any other reason.

would be at the center of percussion or "sweet spot." But I know some players who putt off the toe of the club and some who putt off the heel. If they're good putters, they make contact consistently at that same spot.

The problem is, there is less margin for error toward the heel or toe. Dave Pelz, the putting guru, tells me that if you're trying to hit the ball at the sweet spot and miss a little, there is much less energy loss than if you're hitting it with the toe and miss it the same amount. If you're trying to hit it with the toe and miss it more toward the toe, there will be a lot of energy loss and the club might twist. If you miss it toward the sweet spot, there will be an energy gain, but the putt still won't roll the distance you were planning on. That's the value of toe-and-heel-weighted putters—they are more stable on a mis-hit. There is no advantage on a perfect hit.

So if you can hit it at exactly the same place on the club every time, it doesn't make any difference where that place is. If you can't—and few of us can—it's best to think of using the sweet spot, or at least trying to.

A good practice device to see where you are making contact is to put some chalk on the back of a few balls, hit some putts and look at the markings on the clubface.

By the way, don't be fooled into thinking the sweet spot is always in the center of the clubface, or where the manufacturer puts his mark on the top of the putter. That may or may not be the center of percussion. It varies with the style of putter but is often more toward the heel, especially with heel-shafted putters. You can find out by holding up the putter with your thumb and forefinger at the grip end and flicking the face with a pencil or a finger. When it bounces straight back without twisting, you've found the sweet spot.

A better way is to go to the putting green and hit a few putts. Trust your athletic ability to find the spot on the face of your putter that rolls the ball best.

The putting stroke. As with the full golf swing, there is no "best" way to putt. The most important thing is to have

If you can hit it at exactly the same place on the club every time, it doesn't make any difference where that place is.

It doesn't really matter what you do as long as it's repetitive and you have total confidence in it.

confidence in what you are doing. You can have the purest putting stroke in the world, but if you don't have confidence in it, it's not going to produce the desired results. Or you can have a poorer stroke, but if you have a lot of confidence in it, have an excellent touch and can repeat it often enough, you can be a good putter.

Bobby Locke didn't have a classic putting stroke. It looked like he hooked every putt. But he was one of the greatest putters ever. My dad, Tom Sr., lines up way left and pushes every putt, but he's one of the best amateur putters I've ever seen. So it doesn't really matter what you do as long as it's repetitive and you have total confidence in it and it works.

If you talked to a number of teachers or other experts about who has the perfect putting stroke, some would say Ben Crenshaw, others would say George Archer or Jack Nicklaus or Tom Kite or Lee Trevino or Gary Player. Arnold Palmer in his prime was the best putter around. So was Tom Watson when he was winning. In my opinion, Steve Jones has one of the best putting strokes on Tour today. The interesting thing is that each of them has a different stroke. The important thing is that each makes that same different stroke almost every time.

In the middle of the 1989 season I lost some confidence in my putting method for a period of time. I was not putting well and was looking for something that would work, so I switched to cross-handed, and everybody was shocked. Somebody told me that there had never been a great cross-handed putter. I said, "Yes, there has. I'm a great putter and I putt cross-handed."

I putted well throughout that summer and almost won the U.S. Open putting cross-handed. The fact that I didn't win had nothing to do with my putting. Later in 1989, with my confidence restored, I switched back to the conventional grip and won the Nabisco Championships. At the Bob Hope Classic early in 1990, putting conventionally, I had a terrible time, three-putting five times in the first two rounds. And starting the third round I missed short birdie putts on the first two holes. On the third hole I had had enough and went cross-handed. I played the next seven holes seven under par . . . and putted well the rest of the week. I finished two strokes behind the winner, Peter Jacobsen.

A month or so later I went back to the conventional method, but early in August I switched to cross-handed again and, to satisfy the "doubting Thomases," I hope, won the Federal Express St. Jude Classic in Memphis putting that way. It was a wonderful week of ball hitting and great putting. I shot 15 under par, including a record 62 with 25 putts, and beat John Cook with a birdie on the first playoff hole.

People have had trouble with my switching back and forth because they thought it wasn't logical that I could putt well both ways. These are the same people who would say it's not logical for Michael Jordan to drive underneath, hang in the air for five seconds and make a reverse layup while he's guarded by four guys. Well, who says it has to be logical? I think you play your best when you're not worrying about logic and are being creative. Michael Jordan is simply reacting to a situation, and that's what I do. If I don't feel comfortable the conventional way, I switch to cross-handed. Usually I make a bunch of putts right away.

If I had changed putters, which would have been a more radical change, nobody would have said a word. And I've done that, too. One year at the Mixed Team Classic, a friend of mine was walking around with Vinny Giles, my business manager, watching me and Beth Daniel. My friend noticed that I was using a different putter than the last time he'd seen me, and Vinny said, "He's had four different putters this year . . . and he makes everything with every one of them."

The point is, whatever you putt with or however you putt, you have to have confidence. I've always been a good putter and I probably always will be. It really doesn't matter what putter I'm using or which hand is on top. If I have total confidence in it, I'm going to make a lot of putts.

There *are* some things you have to do with your stroke to satisfy the considerations of solid contact. Most good putting

You play your best when you're not worrying about logic and are being creative.

THE STROKE IS FROM LOW TO HIGHER

The putter should at least be swung low to the ground, and many good putters have a stroke that is slightly ascending through and beyond impact. The ball is hit with the putter-face ideally having zero loft at impact. The hands, arms and shoulders move as a unit, especially on a short putt as shown here.

THE PUTTERFACE SHOULD LOOK DOWN THE LINE

One important factor in making putts is having the putterface looking down the target line at impact. A lot of rotation in the head of the putter during the stroke makes the stroke more difficult to repeat. Although there are many who do it differently, the ideal path for a short putt is straight back and straight through. And the good putters have the face aimed down the target line when they strike the ball.

Try to make your impact position look just like your address position.

clubs have one to four degrees of loft on the face. Therefore, in order to strike the ball with zero loft, you have to have your hands slightly in front of the ball at impact. If you let your wrists break too quickly and flip the face upward through impact, you add loft to the club. That gets the ball slightly in the air and makes it bounce. So I think having your hands slightly ahead of the ball at impact is important. A good thought is to have your hands slightly ahead of the ball at address, then return to that same position at impact, keeping constant whatever angle there is between the shaft and your left arm.

The type of putter you use has an influence on how you make solid contact. Most putters are shallower than the ball, so if the club is on the ground at the point of impact, you will hit the center of the ball somewhere near the top of the face. A deeper putter must be swung so at impact the putterhead is lower to the ground than with a shallower putter. If you are to hit the center of the ball with the center of the club, the clubface will be just slightly off the grass. A shallower putter should be swung a little higher off the ground, a quarter of an inch or so, to get solid contact and a true roll.

The angle at which the putter comes into the ball is important. It should be moving level or *slightly* upward. On fast, smooth greens, especially, you don't want to hit down on the ball. Most times I putt with a shallower, blade-type putter, so I like to feel as if I'm striking the putt with a blow that is almost level to slightly ascending. The putter is swung back low and goes from low to higher on the forward stroke—not a lot higher, but higher. And I don't mean add loft to the putter by flipping it. Keep the face flat as the putterhead swings through the ball on a slightly upward arc. A good thought is to try to make your impact position look just like your address position.

Dave Stockton, one of the best putters ever, believes the putter should be kept low through and after impact. Dave putts with a deeper, mallet-type putter, so he has to have that feeling to keep the putter lower. Jackie Burke was a great putter and he kept the putterhead low after impact. The late Claude Harmon told Curtis Strange to keep it low on the follow-through. Jack Nicklaus, who uses a deeper putter, keeps it low. So do Gary Player and Billy Casper, who often end up with the putter on the ground at the finish of their strokes.

But they all are swinging basically level. They're not hitting down on the ball. It's all done in an effort to hit the center of the ball with the center of the clubface with zero loft.

Isao Aoki once told me that you never want to hit up on a putt, that you always want to hit down. That surprised me, but then I considered that he grew up on Korai greens in Japan. That's a grass even coarser and thicker than common Bermuda, and the ball sits down in it. If you hit up on the ball, it actually drives it farther into the grass and makes it hop. If you hit down on it with a flat face, the ball seems to get up on top of the grass and roll. But remember, you don't want any negative loft with that downward stroke.

So Isao is a product of his environment, as we all are. He's also a wonderful putter on firm, fast greens, which is because he has such wonderful touch and confidence. But nowadays I don't see too many good putters who grew up on fast greens hitting down on the ball. Fine putters like Ben Crenshaw, Paul Azinger, Nick Faldo, Payne Stewart, Greg Norman, Mark Calcavecchia—and Tom Kite—all hit up on it to a certain extent.

I really don't think it matters which side or hand controls the stroke. Ideally the two hands and arms move together. If you tend to overcontrol your stroke with your right hand, you need to think about your left. If you tend to overcontrol with your left, you need to think about your right, just as in the full swing. I feel I putt with the hands, arms and shoulders moving as a unit. There will be some natural action of the hands, of course, as the stroke gets longer. That's the same as in the full swing, except that there should be almost no body movement in putting.

Hit the center of the ball with the center of the clubface with zero loft.

MIMIC ADDRESS POSITION AT IMPACT

There will be some natural action of the hands as the putting stroke gets longer, but the goal is to return your arms, hands and putter to the same position at impact (Frame 4) they were in at address (Frame 1). Again, the face of the putter should be kept flat, with zero loft, as it is swung through the ball on a slightly upward arc.

4

IT'S INSIDE TO INSIDE ON LONGER PUTTS

*The putterhead should start straight back from the ball, but
as the stroke gets longer it will swing inside the target line,
a natural reaction to the turning of your shoulders. On the
forward stroke, the club will return to down the line at
impact, then inside again on the follow-through.*

But there are putters who basically don't move anything at the start of the backswing except their hands. Billy Casper, Arnold Palmer, Jackie Burke—they all just break the club away with their hands. Their hands actually move down as the club goes back, which is what keeps the club low. Sure, there is some arm swing, especially on the longer putts, but the stroke is done mostly with the hands. That's the "pop" method versus the "stroke" method. Casper has been a master at it. He just sets his arms and hands so close to his body that it is difficult for him to move his arms, then hinges the putter back and through. Aoki has an extreme style—he carries his hands very low, sets his putter on the heel with the toe sticking way up in the air and just pops it with his hands.

Jack Nicklaus belongs in an "in-between" group that uses a combination of hand and arm movement, but his hands are definitely active in the stroke.

Players who putt with their shoulders include Bob Charles, one of the best ever; Faldo, Mark O'Meara and Chip Beck.

So there are a lot of ways to do it effectively.

One thing you must do to make putts is have the face of the putter looking down your target line at impact.

One thing you must do to make putts is have the face of the putter looking down your target line at impact. You don't want to have the putterhead rotating too much, because that's difficult to repeat time after time. The more you can keep the blade square and the more you can keep the path of your stroke down the target line, the better chance you have to start your putts on line. Ideally, the path of your stroke should be straight back and straight through on the shorter putts. As the putt gets longer, the putter will move to the inside on the backswing as your shoulders turn, travel down the target line through impact, then go back to the inside after impact.

There are great putters who do it differently. Ben Crenshaw swings the putter way inside going back. Kathy Whitworth always has been a wonderful putter, and she picks it up to the outside. Dave Stockton kind of drags it to the outside, makes a little loop in the swing and comes into the ball from the inside. In fact, Dave once told me that you don't want to take the putter straight back, that you want to have it go a little bit outside or a little bit inside. Much the same as a lot of professionals feel it is difficult to hit a perfectly straight ball and want to curve it in one direction or the other, Dave wants to feel that he is able to hook his putts into the hole.

In their book *The Search for the Perfect Swing,* Alastair Cochran and John Stobbs state that you can't put sidespin on a putt. They say you can't hook or slice it because the ball doesn't stay on the clubface long enough to be compressed. I'm not too sure about that, but I know it's important to have the club moving generally down the line on which you want the putt to start and the face of the putter aimed down that line when you hit the ball.

The putting grip and setup. The first consideration in setting your hands on the putter is that they must oppose each other. If your left hand is more on top of the club than your right, the face will tend to rotate to the left. The opposite is true if the right hand is too much on top. It's the same concept as in the full swing. But in putting you can have your hands more under the club, the left hand turned to the left and the right hand turned to the right.

You're not looking to generate speed with the hands in putting. There can be some hinging action, even if you're an arm-and-shoulder putter, and some release through impact on the longer putts. But what you're after most is *stability.* You don't want the hands rotating.

How much you place your hands under or on top of the shaft isn't really important as long as they oppose each other. Dave Stockton and Ben Crenshaw put their hands in a position where both thumbs run straight down the shaft. Jack Nicklaus, Arnold Palmer and Billy Casper turn their hands about 30 degrees or so underneath the shaft. Paul Runyan turns his hands 45 degrees or more. That's why I really don't think *how much* you do it matters a lot. I've just named six

You're not looking to generate speed with the hands in putting . . . what you're after most is stability.

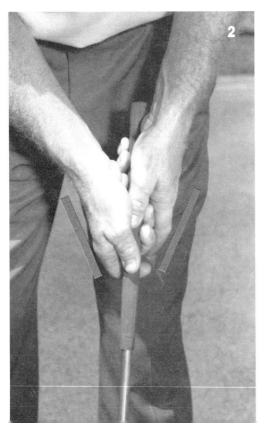

THE HANDS OPPOSE IN PUTTING

The main consideration in gripping the putter is that the hands should be in opposition, each positioned square or under the shaft an equal and opposite amount. The handle of the putter is laid across the heel pad of the left hand (Frame 1). The last three fingers close around the club and the right hand is placed in an opposing position (Frame 2). The forearms and putter hang basically straight down, which makes the wrists slightly arched (Frame 3).

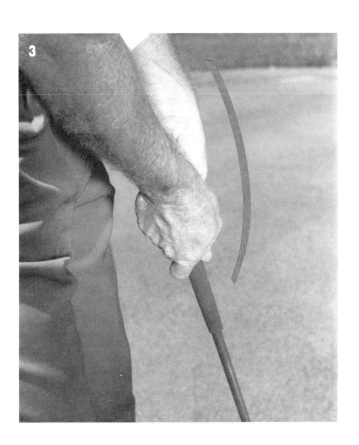

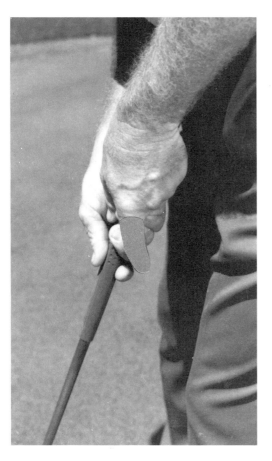

THE LEFT FOREFINGER IS RELAXED

The forefinger of the left hand is laid over the fingers of the right. This is known as the reverse overlap grip, which increases the stability in the back of the left wrist. Stretching the forefinger straight down the shaft increases that stability but also increases tension, so just laying it over the fingers of the right in a relaxed manner is probably the best method. The regular or ten-finger grips can be equally effective.

THE CROSS-HANDED GRIP

This grip, which further increases the stability in the back of the left hand and wrist, is taken exactly as the reverse overlap, except that two hands are reversed. The left hand is below the right and the forefinger of the right hand is laid over the fingers of the left. Again, the cross-handed version of the full-swing or ten-finger grips can work well.

HANDS AHEAD AT ADDRESS

Set your hands slightly ahead of the ball at address. That helps you return them to the same position at impact and hit the ball with zero loft on the putterface. There are many ways to stand to the ball, but the theoretical ideal is to have your weight slightly on the left and equally balanced between the balls and heels of your feet. How straight your arms hang is a function of how erect you stand, the length of your putter and how much your hands are under the shaft—the more they are under, the more your elbows will be bent.

EYES OVER OR INSIDE THE BALL

Your posture—how much you bend over—determines the position of your eyes in relation to the ball. Ideally, your eyes should be over the ball, but many good putters have their eyes set inside the ball. Setting up with your eyes outside the ball promotes trouble. There are good putters who have an open stance, but most players putt better when their shoulders and forearms are square— when lines across them are parallel to the target line.

167

wonderful putters, and the only thing they have in common is the fact that their hands oppose each other, in balance.

I'm probably somewhat like Nicklaus and Casper, with my hands not straight down the shaft but not nearly as much under as a Runyan.

You don't want to put your hands too much *on top* of the club, because that tends to push the shaft down at address and makes it very difficult to sole the club.

How your arms hang at address depends on how erect you stand to the ball, the length of your putter and how much your hands are under the shaft. Crenshaw's arms hang straight down, because he has an erect posture, his putter is only 33 inches long and his hands are pretty much on top of the shaft. Stockton's grip position is about the same as Ben's, but his elbows are bent because his putter is longer and he is more bent over at address.

In general, the more you put your hands under the club, the more your elbows are going to be bent. But that happens naturally.

The most common putting grip is the reverse overlap, in which the forefinger of the left hand is laid over the fingers of the right. It doesn't matter whether you use that style or the standard overlap or the ten-finger grip. The reason most players use the reverse overlap is that they're looking for some stability in the back of the left wrist.

When I was growing up and first started watching golf on TV, Arnold Palmer used the reverse overlap with the left forefinger really extended, pointing straight down the shaft. I thought, "That's good enough for me," and so I used that. But Mr. Penick changed that finger position. Stretching the finger down the shaft does increase the stability of the left hand, but it also creates more tension. He wanted me to just wrap it around the other fingers in a more relaxed position, which is what I do now.

I feel that the pressure in the grip should be with the last three fingers of the left hand and the middle two fingers of the right, just as in the full-swing grip. A number of people including George Low, a great putter and teacher, believe that the thumb and forefinger of the right are very important, that you should actually pinch the shaft between them. I've tried that several times and it doesn't work for me, so I'm not a believer in it, but I don't have any problem with somebody who does it, provided he maintains the opposing position of his hands.

The overall pressure of your grip should be as light as possible—not loose, but light, but it will vary with the speed of the greens. On fast greens you need to have a lighter grip to insure that you can swing the club slowly enough with a rhythmic stroke and hit the ball the proper distance. On slow greens you must swing the club faster and so you instinctively will grip it more firmly to control the club. In all cases, as with the full swing, there should be as little tension as possible in the hands and forearms.

In all cases, there should be as little tension as possible in the hands and forearms.

Your posture can be an individual choice, and you see a lot of different ones on Tour. Personally, I don't advocate an erect posture. I don't feel like I'm down to business if I don't bend over a little bit. But Crenshaw and others do very nicely from a more erect position. The main thing your posture determines is the position of your eyes. In theory, your eyes should be over the ball. That allows you to rotate your head as you look directly down the line. But I see a lot of good putters with their eyes well inside the line. Fuzzy Zoeller's eyes are inside the ball. Crenshaw's eye line is quite a bit inside. Standing that far from the ball is one reason he takes the putter back inside. And few players have ever putted better.

I've never seen a good putter with his eyes set outside the ball. That promotes taking the club back outside and cutting across it coming through. So set your eyes over or inside the ball, never outside.

I prefer a square stance with my weight balanced between the balls and heels of my feet. Stockton believes that a square stance allows you to putt across your body, to maintain a relationship between your hands and body throughout

Reading greens is a learned ability. It's like teaching a young child to throw a ball.

the stroke. He says that with an open stance you're just swinging out into space, lining up left and swinging to the right. Many good putters stand open and swing to the right—Nicklaus and Crenshaw, to name a couple. But most people tend to do better when they're fairly square.

When I talk about a square stance, the most important part of the body to keep square is the shoulders. The feet can be slightly open or closed and it doesn't matter much as long as the shoulders are square. The arms hinge to the shoulders, so if they are square it helps in swinging the arms and putter toward the target.

A good check is to have your caddie or a friend lay a shaft across your forearms or shoulders when you're at address. If the shaft is parallel to your target line, that means your forearms and shoulders are, too, which gives you a good chance to swing the putter straight back and through.

On reading greens. To be honest, I don't think there is any way to tell somebody how to read greens. Reading greens is a learned ability. It's like teaching a young child to throw a ball. You ask him to throw the ball to you, and the first time it falls a few feet in front of you. The next throw goes over your head. But after a few more throws he gets the right distance, because he's developed a feel for it. It's a learning experience.

I can tell you the obvious things. Gravity works. If the slope is from left to right, the putt is going to break to the right. The slope will have more influence and the putt will break more as it begins to slow down. You have to hit an uphill putt harder, a downhill putt easier. But I don't know any shortcut in learning how to do all this except to hit putts. I'll suggest some games in the chapter on practice that will help you learn to read greens, but you simply have to practice and play until you develop a feel for it.

Grain, the way the grass grows, can be a factor in how much the ball breaks and how fast it rolls. The longer and coarser the grass, the more effect it will have. On Bermuda

PRACTICE LONG, BREAKING PUTTS
*Learn to read greens and develop touch at the same time by
hitting long, breaking putts on the practice green. The longer
the putt, the better touch you can develop. Practice putts with
different amounts of break, right to left and left to right,
uphill and downhill, to learn how to do it on the course.*

The ideal is to have a good stroke and totally trust it.

grass I pay a lot of attention to grain. On *Poa annua* I pay a little bit of attention. On really good bent grass in the north I don't pay too much attention at all.

Putts with the grain will roll faster than putts against the grain. Cross-grain will influence the break of a putt. It will break more in the direction the grain is growing, less the opposite way.

There are several ways to figure out the direction of the grain. If the green surface looks shiny, the grass is growing away from you. If it's dull, you're looking into the grain. Examine the cup to see which side is worn. That's the direction in which the grass is growing. If all else fails, the rule of thumb is that grass, especially the coarser varieties, grows toward the setting sun—in the northern hemisphere that's generally toward the southwest. This will be especially true later in the day when the grass is longer.

How to develop touch. Having given you a lot of mechanical advice, let me point out that Harvey Penick always said he would take a man with touch over a man with a perfect putting stroke and no touch any day.

Having touch means having a feel for your stroke and a feel for the greens. Having touch means having trust in your stroke so you can make a relaxed, free swing through the ball. As it is with the full swing, the ideal is to have a good stroke and totally trust it.

Does the fact that you feel your putting stroke is good allow you to free up enough to feel the stroke? Or do you suddenly start feeling the stroke and trusting it and it gets better mechanically? I don't know that there's an answer. We don't have to be logical here. I do know that if you want to free up your stroke, you darned sure don't want a lot of mechanical thoughts running through your mind.

To develop touch you have to practice playing golf. You have to do things in your practice that teach you how to play golf. Training aids like chalk lines, putting tracks and 2 × 4s laid side by side are wonderful for developing your stroke, but they do not help you develop touch. They do help you develop the proper technique, but using them should not be your primary consideration in practice. I see guys on Tour who hit straight 10-footers along a chalk line, putt after putt, hour after hour. That's wonderful if they happen to get a straight-in 10-foot putt on every hole. But that doesn't help them hit a 30-footer the right distance or die a breaking putt into the cup. They are perfecting the stroke, sure, but a perfect stroke does not always make a perfect putter.

You also need to hit a lot of different putts, from different distances and with different breaks. Try to roll the ball at the proper speed and make it go the proper distance. Especially hit long putts, 40 to 60 feet, putts you don't have much chance of making but are trying to get close. This helps you build a feel for the stroke. You seldom will get the ball too far off-line.

Combining putting drills with stroking long putts is the best of both worlds. You're doing the training and the trusting at the same time.

On Tour, we play on smooth, fast greens. You may play on greens with different speeds in your area or, as you travel around the country and around the world, on greens with different speeds and different textures of grass. Despite this, whatever type of stroke you use, stick with it under all conditions. There is no need to change styles to fit the greens.

Adapting to conditions is really pretty easy. The faster the greens, the shorter and slower the stroke must be. The slower the greens, the longer and faster the stroke must be.

Sandra Palmer, one of the great players on the LPGA Tour, once told me about the time she was getting ready for the U.S. Women's Open and was concerned about the greens. She called Mr. Penick and told him she was afraid that she wouldn't be able to handle them because they were so fast. He said, "Well, if the greens are that fast, you probably need to hit it easier."

It's hard to argue with that kind of logic. Develop a good stroke and a good touch and don't change them. Just adapt

Do the training and the trusting at the same time.

The Lord hates a coward ... and he doesn't think much of a fool, either.

them to the various conditions.

Whether you putt boldly or cautiously depends on what the situation, the slope and speed of the green, allows. It also depends to some extent on your personality and your confidence in your stroke at the time. In their primes, players like Arnold Palmer and Tom Watson were famous for charging long putts, sometimes knocking them several feet past the hole. But they had the confidence and the ability to make the putts coming back. Jack Nicklaus always has been an advocate of letting the ball die at the hole, because a ball that's moving more slowly has a better chance of toppling in.

I subscribe to Jack's philosophy. The old "never up, never in" theory gets a lot of golfers in trouble. Sam Snead once was playing with an amateur who rammed a 20-foot putt about 10 feet past the hole. The amateur said, "Well, the Lord hates a coward." To which Sam replied, "And he doesn't think much of a fool, either."

Mr. Penick always said a long putt that stopped an inch short of the hole was better than one that went six feet past, because it was closer to having the proper speed and therefore had a better chance of dropping. The old joke says that 95 percent of putts left short won't go in. Well, neither will 95 percent of the putts that are destined to go six feet past.

Putting the proper speed on a putt depends on touch, which depends on trust and a total lack of anxiety. Ben Crenshaw says all he tries to do is stand over a putt, get as relaxed as possible and then just roll the ball. He describes himself as a "fatalistic" putter and says he doesn't feel too many putts he hits are going to go in.

I feel much the same way. I don't want to get too wrapped up in the putt. I'm just trying to roll the ball and make it start on the line that I picked out, relying on my touch to give it the proper speed. That's all you have control over. You don't have control over whether it goes in.

But both Ben and I have made our share over the years.

CHAPTER 5/ PLAYING FROM TROUBLE

The course record wouldn't have happened if I hadn't been able to pull off the trouble shot.

I was on the 15th hole at Pebble Beach during the third round of the 1983 Crosby. I had pushed my drive to the right and my ball was underneath one of those funky little trees that grow sideways out there. My problem was that I had to hit the ball underneath the trunk of the tree that was right in front of me and still carry the rough so I could get it up in front of the green. Normally it would have required a 4-iron to stay underneath the tree, but I wasn't sure I could get the shot high enough to carry over the edge of the rough.

So I took a 5-iron, put the ball back in my stance a little and played a wonderful little punch shot that stayed under the tree, carried the rough and ended up in front of the green. Then I chipped it in for a birdie. I parred the last three holes and shot 62, the course record at Pebble, then won the tournament the next day. It's a course record I'm proud of, but it wouldn't have happened if I hadn't been able to pull off that trouble shot on 15.

In the second round of the 1986 Masters I hit my second shot into the water hazard in front of the 13th green. I was lucky, because the ball was sitting on a little sandbar, sort of like in a bunker. But the ditch was pretty deep and I had to straddle the water. The pin was on the top left of the green, just over a ridge. I took a wide stance and blasted the ball out, just like a bunker shot. I didn't know if there were rocks underneath the sand or not. Luckily there weren't, and the ball ended up about four feet from the hole. I made it for birdie. I had been looking at 6 and made 4, so that was a big recovery.

The first requirement for successful trouble play is sheer imagination. There is no way you can experience, on the practice tee, every shot you're going to encounter on the golf course. You'll have all kinds of different situations, different stances, different lies to cope with. So imagination and creativity play a tremendous role in recovering from trouble. You must play wisely, but don't play blindly. Don't just accept the obvious way out of the woods. Look for openings in the tree branches or around the trees. Imagine how your ball must fly to get on the green or to the best possible point. The most creative players are the best at it. Seve Ballesteros is a genius out of trouble because he knows how to make the shots and is not afraid to try them. So is Ben Crenshaw.

Having said all that, I'll now tell you that you have to practice as many situations as you can, on the range and on the course. There are certain fundamentals that apply in most trouble situations, so you need to work on those fundamentals and apply them to different shots.

There is an effective way to practice these shots. You play practice. Play games with your friends and with yourself— see how low you can hit the ball, or how high. Curve shots around an object, real or imagined. I'll give you some specific games to play in the next chapter, but you can come up with many on your own. You can do this on the practice tee or on the course, preferably both. I'm sure you can find areas on or around your practice tee where you can hit shots from bare lies, from divots and from rough. And you can go on the course in the evenings, when it's not crowded, and play

> The first requirement for successful trouble play is sheer imagination.

games with yourself or with friends. It's the best way to learn how to play golf.

This won't prepare you for every shot you're going to encounter, but just maybe the shot you're facing right now is similar to one you've been practicing. The more you can make that happen, the better you'll be able to play from trouble.

I'm going to give you my technique for playing from bad lies and bad situations. These are only the fundamentals, and you'll need to apply them to each particular instance, but use your imagination to make them work most effectively.

First, a basic rule. While I encourage imagination and creativity, I don't condone stupidity. The first thing you have to do with any trouble shot is get out of trouble. *You have to avoid the immediate obstacle.* That may mean you can't hit to the green or even forward toward the green, but getting past the obstacle is your first order of business.

So if you're in the rough, you have to get it out of the rough. If you're behind trees, you have to get it out of the trees. If you have to hit over a tree, take enough loft to get it over. Don't be worried about getting to the green until you get over the tree. If you're in a bunker, get it out of the bunker. If you leave it there, you have the same shot all over again.

In all of these situations you may have an opening and a chance to get the ball to the green, but getting it on the green is secondary to getting out of the trouble you find yourself in. Don't turn a one-stroke penalty into two or three.

Getting it on the green is secondary to getting out of the trouble you find yourself in.

How to curve the ball. One of the basic factors in escaping from trouble is your ability to curve the ball in the direction needed when you need it. The old saying, "If you can slice it in you can slice it out" is only true if you can hit that second slice on call.

On the 17th hole at Southwind, in the final round of the 1990 Federal Express St. Jude Classic near Memphis, I hit my drive down the right side of the fairway and had a tree blocking my way to the flag, which was tucked way to the right side of the green. I was trailing John Cook by a stroke. The hole is about a 450-yard par 4, and I had 190 to the pin with a strong right-to-left wind. I took a 3-iron and sliced the ball about 40 yards around the tree to within a foot of the hole. It was probably the best shot I've ever hit in competition. The birdie pulled me into a tie, and I went on to win the tournament with a birdie on the first playoff hole.

This was a major-league slice, but it was by no means the first time I had hit it. As a kid growing up, I competed in contests to see who could hit the biggest slice or hook. And I won a few of those contests. Little did I know at the time that those contests for a bottle of pop would prepare me for the showdown in Memphis with John Cook.

That shot, and others like it, are accomplished primarily by your address position. If you want to fade the ball, aim your clubface at the target and align your body to the left. If you have to hit a big slice, open your clubface a little to the target and line up well to the left. Then swing the club along your stance line. The ball will start generally in that direction and move left to right.

To draw the ball, aim your clubface at the target and align your body to the right. For a big hook, close the clubface a little and line up well to the right. Then swing along your stance line.

A general rule is to aim the clubface where you want the ball to end up and align your body along the line on which you want the ball to start. But I'd suggest you allow yourself plenty of leeway to get around the object in front of you. The tendency is to not trust the alignment of the body and leave the clubface open in the slice swing, thus starting the ball farther to the right than you want, and to instinctively close it in the hook swing. This will start the ball farther left than you intended. So make sure you have plenty of room to get around the object in your way.

Also, a fade or slice will tend to fly higher than normal, because you have effectively added loft to the club, and a

Make sure you have plenty of room to get around the object in your way.

HOW TO SET UP FOR A SLICE

To slice the ball from left to right, set up with an open stance (1), the left side pulled farther away from the target line than the right. Keep the clubface aimed at the target. Then just swing along your stance line. For an exaggerated slice, open the stance even more and open the clubface (2). Be sure now to allow plenty of room to the left of the object you're trying to slice around.

HOW TO SET UP FOR A HOOK

To hook the ball from right to left, set up closed (1), the right side pulled back farther from the target line than the left. Aim the clubface at the target and swing along your stance line. To hit a bigger hook, close the stance more and close the clubface (2). Again, allow a lot of room to get the ball around the object.

181

draw or hook will go lower, because you have deflofted the club. So allow for that in your club selection. If the club you choose for a draw or hook is too straight-faced, you're likely to drive the ball into the ground too soon and not get the distance you need. The opposite is true for a fade or slice. A too-lofted club could get the ball up too quickly and into the tree branches, or else you won't get enough distance on the shot to get to your target.

A low slice and a high hook are among the hardest shots in golf. They can be played, to some extent, by incorporating the ball-position guidelines I'll mention next, but they're risky if you're trying to get under or over trees.

How to hit it high and low. To hit a shot higher than normal with any given club, you must add loft to the club. Therefore the grip end of the club must be behind the clubhead or laying back at impact. One good way to insure this impact position is to play the ball farther forward, more toward the left foot, at address. Set your weight a little more to your right side and feel that your swing is "uppish" through impact (although not so much that you don't make solid contact).

For a lower shot, position the ball back in your stance, set your weight slightly left and swing down and through the ball. Your follow-through should be more forward and abbreviated rather than up and full.

Only practice will teach you how far forward or back you must position the ball to achieve different heights.

Getting out of rough. In line with what I said earlier, the first decision you must make when your ball is in the rough is to choose a club that will get it out of there. The error I see a lot of amateurs making is that they try to get too much out of the shot. They try to knock it on the green without first getting it out of the rough. They forget that the obstacle is right there in front of them, and they try to advance the ball too far. Generally, they hit too many woods and too many long irons out of heavy grass. That ends up costing them. They often leave the ball in the rough and compound the problem.

So assess your lie. Determine how thick or tough the rough is and how far down your ball is buried in it. When the ball is sitting down in the rough, it's played just like a buried bunker shot—you have to get the club down to the ball. If you don't, you're not going to get it out.

Learn what you can do with various clubs from various lies. Sometimes you can hit a 7-iron farther than a 6-iron because the loft of the club may help you get it up and out of the grass more quickly.

Sometimes, especially if the ball is not deep in the grass, a lofted fairway wood is the best play out of rough. The broad sole and mass of the clubhead help it slide through the grass more easily. And because the wood is constructed differently than the iron, there is less chance that grass will get wrapped around the hosel and twist the club closed.

That last factor is something to watch out for in the rough. If the grass is particularly wiry or heavy, there is a tendency for the club to twist closed through impact. In this situation, it's usually a good idea to set the iron club a little open at address as a countermeasure.

The technique for getting the club down to the ball in the rough is pretty simple. Set your weight a little more on your left side and cock your hands up a little earlier on the backswing. This makes the swing steeper and gives you more of a descending blow coming down. That helps the club get down and through the ball better.

But remember the first rule is to get the ball out before you try to advance it farther.

Playing from slopes. Playing shots from uphill, downhill and sidehill lies is simply a matter of adjustment in the way you address the ball and aim the shot.

On uphill and downhill lies, try to align your shoulders as much as you can with the slope. On an uphill lie, your weight will fall more to the right, which will set your shoulders and

> The error I see a lot of amateurs making is that they try to get too much out of the shot.

SWING STEEPER OUT OF THE ROUGH

To escape from the rough, you have to get your club down to the ball. Usually an iron (above) with enough loft to get the ball out of the grass is the best play. Set the blade open slightly, put your weight a little more on your left side and cock your hands up more quickly on the backswing to pro-

duce a steeper backswing and a more descending blow coming down. If the rough is not too high or if the ball is sitting up in the grass, a wood (below) can be effective, because it will slide through the grass more easily.

the rest of your body more in line with the slope. On a downhill lie, the weight will go more to the left and your shoulders will tilt more to the left or downhill.

In each case, try to swing more with the slope. Uphill, swing the club up more. Downhill, chase the club down the slope as much as possible. In general, the ball will be positioned farther forward on an uphill lie, farther back in your stance going downhill. One way to find the best position is to take practice swings and see where your club hits the turf. Then position the ball there.

From an uphill lie, the ball will tend to go higher and shorter and a little left. The downhill shot will travel lower and farther, because you have effectively taken loft off your club, and it will tend to slide a little right. So you might want to allow for these tendencies with your club selection and aim.

The sidehill slopes will accentuate the direction the ball flies. Just as with the sand shots I discussed earlier, if the ball is above your feet it will go to the left, below your feet to the right. How much, of course, depends on the severity of the slope, but you must aim to allow for it.

With the ball above your feet, stand a little taller so you can swing a little more like a batter in baseball. If the slope is extremely severe, try gripping down on the club to control your swing better. Your swing will be flatter or more around your body.

If the ball is below your feet, flex your knees more and maybe bend more from the hips to get down to it. Your swing will naturally be more upright, but let your setup dictate how upright it is.

Coping with bare lies. If your ball is on bare dirt or hardpan, chances are it is sitting cleanly, so you really don't have to chance your technique a lot. The major consideration is to catch the ball first. If you feel like you might have a little trouble doing that, play the ball back a little in your stance. Put your hands a little farther forward and make sure you really hit down on the ball.

Most amateurs don't realize that you really have a big margin for error with this shot, especially if the ground is really hard. If you hit behind it a little, the club will tend to skid into the ball and you'll probably get a pretty good shot anyway.

Again, these shots take some practice to build confidence and to learn how far the ball will travel with a swing of any given length and speed.

Hitting from divots. When your ball rolls into a divot, and after you finish mentally cursing the player who didn't replace the turf, you face a shot where the ball is sitting down. Anytime that happens you have to get the club down to the ball. So play the ball back in your stance, put your hands a little forward and make a steeper swing, cocking the club up more abruptly with your hands. Then drive the clubhead down and through the ball.

Your choice of a club here depends on the depth of the divot and whether the ball is sitting in the middle of it or up against the front lip (if it's against the back lip, a rare occurrence, you now have big problems). Remember, your first priority is to escape, so take a club with enough loft to let you do that.

Splashing from water. Playing a shot out of water is pretty risky. There's really no rule on how much of the ball is underwater before the shot is unplayable and it becomes better to drop and take your penalty. So much of your ability to do that is dependent on your strength. The water is going to kill the speed of the club very quickly, much faster than sand does in a bunker. So you're going to have to swing harder to get the club to move through the water and propel the ball out.

If the ball is just partially submerged, you have a pretty good shot at getting it out. If it's totally submerged, but just barely, you may have a chance. But if a ball is a couple of

SWING WITH THE SLOPES

On uphill and downhill lies, set your shoulders in line with the slope as much as possible. On an uphill lie (above), your weight will fall more to the right side tilting your shoulders more to the right. The ball will be positioned farther forward in your stance. Then try to swing up the slope. On a downhill

188

lie (below), your weight will fall more to the left and your shoulders will tilt more in that direction. The ball should be played farther back in your stance. Then swing along the slope, chasing the clubhead down the hill.

ADJUST YOUR AIM FOR SIDEHILL LIES

When the ball is above your feet, stand a little taller. Your swing will be flatter, more around your body. The ball will go left—the amount depending on the severity of the slope—so adjust your aim for that. With the ball below your feet, flex your knees more and bend more from the hips to get down to it. Your swing will naturally be more upright. The ball will slide to the right, so aim accordingly.

192

5

6

HIT DOWN ON THE BALL IN A DIVOT

The shot from a divot is like any other shot where the ball is sitting down. You have to get the club down to it. Position the ball back in your stance, put your hands a little forward of the ball and make a steeper swing, cocking the club up with your hands and hitting down sharply. Drive the clubhead down and through the ball. Be sure to select a club with enough loft to get the ball out.

The water is going to kill the speed of the club very quickly, much faster than sand does in a bunker.

inches underwater, it's very difficult to catch it perfectly with enough speed to get it out. It's also sometimes difficult to tell where the ball really is, because the water can distort your vision.

A lot of the success with the shot from water depends on what the ball is resting on. The tendency is to hit down underneath the ball, and if there is mud down there your club may get caught up in it and slowed down. Then you have the same shot to hit all over again.

The technique—what technique there is—is basically the same as for the plugged lie in sand. Again, you have to get the club down to the ball. So make a steeper swing and slam the clubhead down behind the ball. Just stick it into the water behind the ball without trying to make a follow-through.

Remember, just as in the sand, you can't touch the water with your clubhead before making your swing. You can't ground your club at any time within the lines of a hazard.

Shots like this usually are gambles, and they don't always pay off. Curtis Strange tried to play his ball out of the water in front of the 13th green in the last round of the 1985 Masters. It didn't come out, he ended up making 6 and lost the tournament by two strokes.

But sometimes they do pay off. If the reward is worth the risk in your particular situation, go ahead and try it. I once saw Jack Nicklaus' second shot on the 15th at Augusta hit the bank in front of the green and roll back into the water. There used to be a little ledge around the edge of the water (it's not there anymore), so the ball might be in the water but you could still play it. Nicklaus took off his right shoe and sock, rolled up his pant-leg, waded in, played the ball out and made birdie.

I also heard of one of our Tour players, who shall remain nameless, who took off his *left* shoe and sock, rolled up his left pant-leg . . . and stuck his right foot into 12 inches of water.

If you're going to attempt this shot, remember that the

CATCH THE BALL FIRST FROM A BARE LIE

*The shot from bare dirt or hardpan doesn't require much
change in your normal technique because it is sitting cleanly.
Try to catch the ball first. As insurance, you can play the ball
slightly back, set your hands a little forward and hit down on
the ball.*

195

HARDPAN PROVIDES A MARGIN FOR ERROR
If you think you might have trouble catching the ball cleanly from hardpan, don't panic. It's better to hit a little behind the ball than to top it, because the hard ground usually allows you some error. The club will tend to skid into the ball and a pretty good shot will usually result.

first priority is always to make sure you bare the correct foot.

Escaping fairway bunkers. I go back to the first rule of trouble play—your first consideration is to get the ball out of the bunker. Then try to advance it as far as you can. So examine your lie and the height of the bunker lip and take a club with enough loft to get it over that lip. You might hit a solid shot with the club that will get you to the green, but if it hits the lip of the bunker, it's not going to get you there.

Choosing the right club, then, is your most important decision. In that regard, the caddies on Tour have an expression—"wood in the sand means wood in the head." I don't choose to hit many woods out of fairway bunkers. I have to have an exceptionally good lie with almost no lip at all before I'll even think about hitting a wood. I'll use irons almost all the time.

The lie is critical to what kind of shot you can play. If the ball is sitting cleanly on top of the sand, you can play the shot conventionally—without grounding your club at address, of course. Make sure your feet are firmly planted and pick the ball off the sand with a normal swing. Or you can open your stance slightly and play a left-to-right cut shot. This helps keep you from catching any sand between the club and the ball.

If the ball is sitting down in the sand, you have to go down and get it. That may mean you're going to hit sand first, a blasting type of shot. So you won't hit it as far, probably not as far as you need to hit it to get to the green.

So be it. It may take a 3-iron to get to the green, but if you don't have a lie that allows you to hit a 3-iron, then don't hit it. Choose a 6- or 7- or 8- or 9-iron, whatever it takes, and get the ball out of the bunker. Then play the next shot. Don't compound your problems by getting greedy.

It's not a question of playing conservatively. It's a matter of playing intelligently.

Intelligently is the way all shots from trouble should be played.

If you're going to play this shot, always make sure you bare the correct foot.

THE LIE IS YOUR GUIDE IN A FAIRWAY BUNKER

The shot you can play from a fairway bunker is dictated by how the ball is sitting in the sand. If the ball is sitting cleanly, you can play a pretty normal shot, making sure your footing is firm and picking the ball off the sand. Opening your stance and playing a left-to-right shot helps you pick the ball cleanly. If the ball is sitting down a little, you may have to catch the sand first, which means you won't get the distance you need. But your first object is to get out. This means you have to be sure to take a club with enough loft to get the ball over the lip.

CHAPTER 6/ HOW TO PLAY PRACTICE

I had played consistently good golf. And I was proud of that.

The decade of the '80s didn't exactly dawn brilliantly for Tom Kite. I did win the European Open in 1980, but I didn't win on our Tour and I fell to 20th on the money list.

In 1981, however, it all came together. Early in March I birdied two of the last three holes to beat Jack Nicklaus in the American Motors-Inverrary Classic, my first PGA Tour win in three years. The next week I almost won at Doral, finishing two strokes back in fourth place.

A little problem with food poisoning just before the Tournament Players Championship the following week set me back for a while, but I had recovered by the time of the Masters, where I finished fifth. Except for the U.S. Open, where I was 20th, I didn't finish lower than eighth the rest of the year.

In 26 starts, I finished in the top ten 21 times, including three thirds, three seconds and a first. I did not miss a cut.

I won the Vardon Trophy with a 69.8 scoring average, the fifth lowest in history, and I was 1981's leading money-winner with $375,699, the first player to become No. 1 with only one victory. I was voted Player of the Year by the Golf Writers Association and played in my second straight Ryder Cup Match. I helped account for three and a half points in a U.S. victory at Walton Heath, just outside London. In winning my singles match against Sandy Lyle I was ten under par for 16 holes.

I ranked seventh or better in six of the Tour's nine statistical categories—seventh in driving accuracy, sixth in sand saves, fifth in percentage of greens hit, fifth in par-breaking percentage, second in birdies and first in scoring. I was 14th in putting, and none of the other top 15 players in greens hit finished that high in the putting category.

No, one victory was not enough. I wanted more, and I had a chance throughout the year to get more. In my three second-place finishes—at Memphis, the World Series and the B.C. Open—I shot final rounds of 68, 67 and 69. But somebody played better each time. It was very hard to win on Tour. It's gotten even harder as the years have gone by.

But I had played consistent golf—make that consistently *good* golf. And I was proud of that.

My 1981 season makes a point. To play consistent golf you have to do reasonably well in every facet of the game. Now, I don't think I'm the best in any category, and if you go down the statistics you see that. I'm not the best driver of the ball, even though I'm very good. I'm not the best at hitting greens in regulation, although I'm usually close. I'm not the best bunker player, but I'm always good. I'm not the best chipper, but I'm a good chipper. I'm not the best putter, but I'm a good putter.

What it amounts to is that I don't really have any glaring weaknesses in my game. That goes back to the fact that Harvey Penick always encouraged us to spend a certain amount of time on each part of our game. He knew that sooner or later we were going to encounter every kind of shot, and when we did he wanted us to have a legitimate chance of executing it.

To play consistent golf you have to do reasonably well in every facet of the game.

It's very easy to practice the things you do well. It's hard to practice the things you have trouble with.

Mr. Penick wanted us to work on what we needed to work on. It's very easy to practice the things that you do well. It's hard to practice the things you have trouble with. It's hard to want to practice bunker shots if you're a pitiful bunker player. It's embarrassing, and you don't want to do it. But that's what you have to do if you're ever going to become a better bunker player.

The pros know this, but I see a lot of amateurs who don't want to work on their weaknesses. If they have trouble with the full shots but are good putters, you'll usually find them on the putting green instead of on the practice tee working on their deficiencies. They take the easy way out, but if you're serious about your game, you have to do just the opposite.

Become proficient in all phases of the game. That way, when one of your wheels begins to slip—and there are times when everybody will putt the ball poorly or drive the ball uncontrollably—you have something to fall back on to compensate for whatever has gone sour.

That's what Mr. Penick made us do, and I'm certain it's one of the big reasons for my consistency.

MAKE YOUR PRACTICE FUN

I have a reputation as a legendary practicer, and I guess I am. But people talk about how hard Tom Kite *works* on his game, and that's not true. Tom Kite *plays* at his game. When I go to the practice tee, I play practice. When I go to the golf course, I play golf.

Practice was never work when I was growing up, and it's not work now. Even when I'm hitting the ball poorly and get frustrated, it's not work. It's fun to try to put the puzzle together. I love to practice, and I think the thing that made me enjoy it so much was the approach Mr. Penick took. He invented games for us to play on the practice tee. We played golf on the golf course and we played practice on the practice tee. And it was wonderful. You're never impatient, it's never work, when you're having fun. The more fun you can have, the more creative you are and the better job you do. And you never get tired. I do better when I take that approach, and you will, too.

Unfortunately, that's not the way many golfers do it. Raised in the work ethic, they work at a game that's supposed to be fun. They say, "Let's go to the practice tee and *work* on our games." Then they say, "Let's go to the course and *play* golf." In a sense, that's fine, but that's usually not what happens. They go to the range and work on their games, then they go to the course and continue to work on their games. And when they come in their scores aren't very good and their tails are dragging. They're tired, because they've been working all day instead of playing.

You want to improve your golf swing to get better, but if you're working at improving it on the golf course, you're not going to make much of a score.

Mr. Penick's No. 1 priority was to teach us to play. He wanted us to practice like we played and play like we practiced. He emphasized that everything we did on the practice tee was to be like playing.

For example, he never wanted us to pull a ball out of the pile and position it in a good lie just in front of a divot, or behind the divot, as many players do. He didn't want us to practice something that we would seldom see on a golf course. The odds against a ball rolling through a divot and perching just on the edge of that divot are so tremendous that you might only see it a dozen times in a lifetime. So why practice it? A golf ball, being round, will tend to roll into a low spot, so you ought to practice that shot. You can't touch it on the golf course, so why should you touch it on the practice tee?

Mr. Penick wanted us to simply tap a ball out of the pile and play it from wherever it ended up. If it rolled into a divot, hit it out of the divot. If it rolled into a perfect lie, hit it from there. When you hit as many practice shots as I did, you've got a lot of divots out there. I hit a lot of shots out of divots when I was growing up. But that surely made the lies

> He wanted us to practice like we played and play like we practiced.

on the course look like the ball was on a tee.

That approach is not the best for a beginner who is trying to learn the fundamentals of the swing. He or she needs a good lie, even to the point of putting the ball on a tee, to avoid getting discouraged. But as that beginner starts to swing better and gets out on the golf course to play, the need arises to learn to hit the ball out of whatever lie is found out there.

Mr. Penick was teaching people how to play golf instead of just teaching them how to swing a golf club. He got his students into a play mentality. That's what I'm trying to do in this book.

You have to practice with a purpose, of course. Certainly you have to practice the fundamentals of your setup, your preshot routine and your swing. The more you practice the easier it is to repeat what you're doing. But if you practice solely to become dependent on swing thoughts, that's not efficient practicing. You practice so you can forget all that once you get on the course.

What are the most important areas of the game to practice? I spend about 60 percent of my practice time on the full game and 40 percent on the short game. You should adjust those percentages, depending on your strengths and weaknesses. But be sure to spend a lot of time on your weaknesses. After that, there are certain clubs you must practice.

Mr. Penick said he always felt like the three most important clubs in the bag, in order of their importance, were the putter, the wedge and the driver. He once asked Ben Hogan what he thought the three most important were, in order, and Hogan said the driver, the putter and the wedge. Mr. Penick said that was close enough. And you have to remember that Hogan didn't miss many greens. About the only time he had to use the wedge was on par-5 holes.

In whatever order you put them, those are your three most important clubs, by far. You have to be able to putt, you have to be able to drive the ball and you have to play good wedge shots. You have to play those three clubs very well.

If you practice solely to become dependent on swing thoughts, that's not efficient practicing.

So practice with those clubs . . . a bunch.

Your purpose in practice is twofold. You want to develop your mechanical skills, and after that you want to develop a feel for your swing and a feel for the shots you're going to have to make on the golf course. You do the training on the practice ground so you can develop the trust on the course.

You go from the swing thought to the feel by hitting different shots. You play practice. You play games, you play golf, on the practice tee. Pretend there's a shot you need for the fourth or fifth hole on the course and hit that shot a few times. Picture having to go over a tree or hooking around it. Hit some bunker shots to different targets as if you were on the golf course. Don't just hit 20 bunker shots in a row to the same target. Chip shots to different holes, one at a time. Practice different putts, make them go different lengths and speeds and tell yourself they count.

How much time you need to spend on mechanics and how much on developing feel depends a lot on your makeup and your approach to the game. When Ben Crenshaw and I were growing up, Mr. Penick took totally different approaches in teaching us. In fact, he never let either of us watch while he was giving the other a lesson.

Mr. Penick was never so sophisticated that he told us to think with the right side or the left side of the brain. That's a subject I'll get into more in the last chapter. But since coming on Tour and having the opportunity to work with some sports psychologists, I've realized that he was teaching us that you play golf best out of the right side, the creative side, of your brain.

Ben was very creative, an awesome talent, and not analytical at all. He just loved to play golf, and he took a right-brained approach to it. He had some mechanical flaws, but he sure could play.

I was more analytical—maybe inquisitive is a better word—about the golf swing and what makes it tick. I loved to play golf, too, but I also loved to practice. I was interested in the mechanics, which I guess is the left-brained or analyti-

He was teaching us that you play golf best out of the creative side of your brain.

The more I practice playing, the better I play.

cal approach.

So Mr. Penick would always encourage Ben to go to the practice tee and practice. If he wouldn't go to the practice tee, Mr. Penick would encourage him to go to the course and play nine holes by himself, playing three or four balls. He'd ask him to hit two balls and play the worst ball. Or play three balls and count the total score. In effect, he was making Ben practice on the course, where Ben wanted to be. He was making him hit a lot of shots under play conditions in a short period of time.

When Mr. Penick gave me a lesson or watched me hit some balls, he would ask me to hit this shot and that shot, and he would warn me never to hit 30 or 40 drivers in a row. When I took a lesson from him, I don't think I ever hit more than five or six shots in a row with the same club. He was making me play golf on the practice tee.

Afterward, he would encourage me to go to the course immediately and see if I could hit the same shots there, playing one ball. He knew I could spend hours on the practice tee without batting an eye. He wanted me to hit good shots on the course, where it counted.

It's still true today. The more I practice playing, the better I play.

Mr. Penick is a genius. I can't imagine any other teacher in the world who has had two such diversified students, personality-wise and in their approaches to the game, as he had in Ben and me and still allowed both to become successful. I think many teachers would have stifled one of those students, but he handled it perfectly. He took a creative player and encouraged him to pay more attention to his mechanics, yet he let him be creative on the course. He took a mechanical player and showed him how to be more creative, both on the practice tee and on the course. If you can recognize your tendencies, that's what you should do with yourself.

Any player who has played a little bit, no matter the caliber of his swing, is better off playing with the right side of the brain—creatively, as opposed to thinking about his swing.

That will produce the best score.

You have to know how and when to practice. You should try to improve your swing, and you do that on the practice tee. But you cannot be practicing when you're on the golf course. There are two distinct methods and thought processes that apply, and they're both necessary to achieve your maximum potential, but they should occur at two distinct times and places. Just be aware that the only reason you're trying to improve your golf swing is so you can take it on the golf course and score better. At some point you have to be able to free up your swing, trust it and let it go.

Practice your mechanics, then blend them into a feel that will help you hit better shots and make better scores.

Every once in a while, after you've learned your basics, you can put a new shot in your repertoire, and if you practice it enough it will work and help you score better. But when you start adding too many of them too quickly, you dilute your consistency, because you're not able to practice the basics.

Don't make the game more complicated than it has to be by throwing in a bunch of stuff that's not important. Don't try to play shots you can't play. And try to play the shots you *can* play as well as possible.

A statement I hear often is, "Gosh, I can do it on the practice tee but I can't do it on the golf course." Well, maybe you're doing different things. Maybe your thought processes are not the same. Maybe you're taking the easy way out on the practice tee and not practicing the things you will encounter on the course. You're not practicing what you play. Or you're not playing what you practice.

Let me list some ways to turn that around.

The only reason you're trying to improve your golf swing is so you can take it on the golf course and score better.

PRACTICE AS YOU PLAY

First let me tell you when *not* to practice. Don't practice when you're tired. When you get tired during a practice session, quit, or at least go to the short game or something less strenuous. At the same time, the change may refresh you mentally. When you're tired, it's difficult to concentrate, and if you're not concentrating you don't want to be practicing.

Fatigue can be physical, depending on the shape you're in, but a lot of times it's more mental. You have to be wanting to do what you're doing, to have it come easy. Otherwise, practice can't be productive or fun. And fun is what you're trying to have while you're getting the desired results.

For most amateurs—and some professionals, for that matter—the big difference between practice and play is that you practice with freedom. If you miss a shot, you can always drag another ball over. Because you have another ball there, it's not going to cost you a shot. When you get on the golf course, you get tight, because you don't have that luxury. This shot is the one that's going to count, and you don't get a second chance. So anxiety sets in.

I have an amateur friend who has trouble with short wedge shots. He's confessed to me that he has a particular problem with tight lies, or even lies on closely mown fairway. My first advice to him was to find some tight lies, drop down a bunch of balls and hit wedge shots until he became fairly proficient at them. I told him not to get analytical. Just hit the shots and watch them to develop a feel for them. That would determine whether he had a physical or technical problem.

He said he didn't think it was physical, that he could hit practice balls onto a fairway in the evenings, then go out and pitch them back to his bag with good success. But he couldn't do the same thing on the course.

His problem is that he isn't practicing as he plays. He isn't practicing what he needs. There is no point in wasting your time by going out and creating a situation that you're not going to find on the course. His attitude is not the same when he can drag another ball over and set it in a perfect lie. He's not likely to get that perfect lie on the course, so the pressure will be greater. The only reason to practice is so you can play on the course.

There are a couple of ways to solve my friend's problem,

The big difference between practice and play is that you practice with freedom.

or yours if you have a similar one. Instead of dropping 40 balls and hitting them, put down just one ball, determine a target 40 yards away and hit that one ball. Then walk out and hit the ball back to where you started. There is no reason to hit 40 balls at a time if you take the attitude that if you miss a shot you have another one. On the golf course you don't have that other one. Practice as you play.

If playing one ball at a time is not convenient in your practice situation, dump out 40 balls or so and hit them to different targets. But tell yourself that you're going to make every one of those shots count. Don't give yourself a perfect lie every time. Just tap it over and play it from where it ends up. Then be very disciplined with every shot. Go through the routine that you're going to go through on the course.

Line up the shot, go through your setup procedure and concentrate. Play the shot and make it count. Tell yourself that this is the only shot you have on this hole and you have to get it close. That may feel a little hokey at first, and maybe out of those 40 balls you'll only hit a few well. That's as opposed to hitting most of them well when you just drag one after another over in front of you and don't approach it the way you would on the course.

In time, however, playing each shot as you would on the course will become more natural. Eventually you will get more and more close. When you can do that, approaching each shot as you would on the course, there's a pretty good chance that when you actually get on the course you're going to be able to do the same thing. Your confidence level will be high, because you've already proved to yourself you can play the shot when it counts . . . even if was only pretending.

Don't feel that you're putting more pressure on yourself on the practice tee. This will take pressure off, because you'll get used to hitting each shot as if it counts. And it will take pressure off on the golf course, when you face a similar shot, because now you'll be used to it. The No. 1 priority is to trust, to have confidence in something that produces the desired result. If what you're using at the moment is not

Don't waste your time by creating a situation you're not going to find on the course.

If what you're using at the moment is not working, then change it until you find something that does work.

working, then change it until you find something that does work. If you have the yips, if your problem is more mental than physical and it means making a mental change, then change your mental approach. Do something different in your thought processes that allows you to hit the shots the way you want. Approaching them as you have to approach each shot on the course is probably the best way to make that change.

That same rule holds true whether your problem is with the putter or the driver or anything in between. Make each shot count in practice, build trust in your method as you simulate play conditions, and you'll find it much easier to execute successfully on the course.

Practicing this way should be fun. Here's how.

GAMES TO PLAY IN PRACTICE

The purpose behind playing games on the practice tee, or while you're practicing on the course, is to do the things that you may encounter during a round of golf. It's difficult to imagine something and almost impossible to accomplish it if you've never experienced it.

According to an article in *Golf Digest*, Ken Green, one of the better players on Tour and one of our freer spirits, once opened the sliding glass door of his hotel room and proceeded to hit 1-iron shots from the carpet through the open door.

That's pure Ken Green, but it's also pure imagination. Ken Green now can go out on the golf course, and when he has to thread a long iron between two trees, and the opening is wider than that sliding glass door, he knows he can do it, because he's done it.

It's not a practice procedure I'd recommend, unless you have a lot of liability insurance. But you can play games like that, hopefully safer, to build your arsenal of shots that you will need on the course.

When I was learning under Mr. Penick, he gave us a lot of games that would make practice more enjoyable. He called it "just piddlin' around." Most of them had to do with the short game, but there were other games that taught us full-swing shots. They are games you can play in competition with one or more friends—Crenshaw and I used to spend hours in the bunkers and around the practice green. You can play for matchsticks or a couple of dollars, if that's your inclination, satisfying your competitive instincts while you're developing your skills and having fun, all at the same time. Or you can compete against yourself.

There was a forked tree in my backyard about 15 feet from our neighbor's fence. I'd throw some balls down a few feet from the tree and try to pop them through the fork so they would come down softly without going into the neighbor's yard, where there was a big Doberman lurking. I'm afraid the dog ate more golf balls than dog food, but I got better.

So piddle around. You can get better, too.

Full-swing games. These are games that will increase your proficiency with the long shots and tell you just what you can do with the various clubs in your bag.

Find your distance. This is not exactly a game, but it's vital to your being able to score effectively. You have to know how far you hit each club in your bag. Use the yardage markers on your practice range if you know they are accurate. Better yet, go on the course when no one is around and stay out there until you hit your best shot with each particular club. Then step it off. Or station somebody out there to measure it for you. Find out what your maximum distance is.

Then give yourself a small target at that distance and see how many balls you can get close to that target. That may remind you that you seldom hit your absolutely best shot on the golf course. Golf is a game of effective misses, so take that into consideration in your club selection.

Find out how far you can hit any given club. See how far that club goes, how far it carries and how far it rolls.

Hit partial shots. Most players only have one swing speed, which makes it difficult to adjust distance when they're in between clubs, which they usually are. It's like learning to

I'm afraid the dog ate more golf balls than dog food, but I got better.

Golf is a game of effective misses, so take that into consideration in your club selection.

ride that bike you got for your sixth birthday. Once you learn it you never forget. But when you got that ten-speed bike on your 12th birthday, you had to learn to shift the gears to get more efficient usage out of it. It's the same with the golf swing. Just because a person can hit a 6-iron 165 yards doesn't mean he knows how to add a little bit to that 6-iron, or take a little bit off. So he's not as effective until he does learn.

Degrees of athletic ability vary, of course. If you don't have great athletic ability, you're not going to be able to do quite as many things with a club as a professional can. But within your capabilities you can learn to hit shots different distances with the same club. It's just a question of practicing enough.

So see how short you can hit any given club. Can you hit a 5-iron 100 yards with a full swing? The top players can do it by varying the speed of their swings. Learn how to vary your distance by taking some lazy swings as well as full, hard ones.

Practice like this helps smooth out your tempo. It also gives you more partial shots that will let you hit the ball closer to the hole. If you've never hit an easy shot, then you never have an easy shot. You always have a hard one.

Hit it high. Go out on the course when it's not crowded and find a barrier—a tree usually is best—and try to hit shots over it. You can start with any club and keep moving closer to see how high you can hit it. It will give you a feel for the natural height of your shot with the various clubs and also will help you learn how much higher you can hit each one.

Hit it low. This is the same game as the high shot but in reverse. Keep moving back as far as you can and see what club you can hit under a tree limb or other object and still carry it close to the green. Hit your normal shot, then close down the clubface and see how low you can hit it with different clubs.

Curve your shots. Find a tree or other object and curve shots around them with various clubs. See how high and how low you can hit a slice. Do the same with a hook. See where you have to start the ball to get it around the object. See how much you can slice shots with different clubs and how much you can hook them. A straighter-faced club will produce more curvature than a more-lofted club, but you need to find out for yourself just how much, so you can choose the right club and aim the ball correctly when you have to curve the ball during a round.

Pick out an intermediate target about 50 yards in front of you—choose a yardage marker on the range or a bush or flag or stick your umbrella in the ground—and see if you can start the ball over it. Start the ball to the left of the object and fade it around. Then start it to the right and draw it around.

Practice curving the ball to different targets. Earlier I mentioned the canisters on our practice range at The Austin Country Club. I would start a shot at one canister and fade it to another, or do the same thing with a draw. Pick out spots on your practice range and do the same. Learning to hit these shots can help you get to pins that are tucked behind bunkers or in other difficult spots.

Practice bad lies. Hit shots out of divots and off bare lies. Watch how the ball reacts. Try to curve the ball off a bare lie, or even out of a divot. Find some rough, either around the practice tee or in an out-of-the-way spot on the course and find out how best you can escape it. Not every lie you get on the course will be perfect. In fact, few of them will be.

Practice from fairway bunkers. Go on the course when no one is around and hit shots from fairway bunkers. Experiment with different clubs from bunkers with different lip heights, and from different positions in the bunker, to find out the least-lofted club that will get you over the lip.

And rake the bunker when you're finished, of course, in case the grounds crew doesn't do it first thing in the morning.

Swing with your feet together. This is more of a drill than a game, but you can make it fun by seeing what kind of different shots you can hit with your feet together. See how far you can hit different clubs, including the driver, see how much you can curve your shots . . . all without falling down. It's

If you've never hit an easy shot, then you never have an easy shot. You always have a hard one.

CURVE YOUR SHOTS

*Find a target, in this case an umbrella staked about 50 yards
in front of you. Start your shots left of the umbrella (top) and
curve them to the right of it, then start them right (bottom)
and curve them to the left.*

HIT SHOTS HIGH AND LOW

Find a tree and hit shots over it (left). Start with any club and keep moving closer to see how high you can hit it. Then hit shots under a limb (right). Keep moving back and see what club you can hit under a limb from a particular distance.

another wonderful way to help out your tempo and improve your balance.

Driving games. There are many games you can play with a driver, one of those three most important clubs. See how short you can hit it with a full swing. Take the club back your usual length and see how smoothly you can hit the ball. See how well you can hit the ball when you tee it up really high—put it on a pencil to exaggerate the height. See how well you can hit it teed really low, much lower than you normally would tee it. See if you can hit some drivers off the ground.

See how high you can hit the ball with a driver and how low you can hit it. See how much you can slice it and how much you can hook it. And see how straight you can hit it.

All these games will increase your control over the club. Even on the course, not every tee shot should be dead straight down the middle, because not every hole is dead straight.

Games on the course. These are games you can play by yourself or with a friend, for money or for bragging rights.

Odd and even. When we were growing up, Mr. Penick had us take just half a bag of clubs when we went out to play nine holes in the afternoon. One day you take the odd-numbered clubs, the next day the evens. It's an excellent way to develop some versatility in your shotmaking. In other words, you learn to hit a 6-iron shot even when you don't have 6-iron.

Call-shot. This is an excellent game with a buddy. You call the shot your friend has to hit—start it toward the left trees and cut it back to the center of the fairway, or start it over the right bunker and draw it in to the flag. If he doesn't do it, it costs him a nickel or a dollar or a bottle of pop when you get in. Don't be too tough on him, though, because he gets to do the same thing to you.

Play your own scramble. Hit three balls, then hit the next three from where the best shot finished and see how low you can score. Or play two balls and play your worst ball and keep score. In this game it does you no good to make a 20-

Not every tee shot should be dead straight down the middle, because not every hole is dead straight.

216

HIT WITH YOUR FEET TOGETHER

Hit different shots with your feet together. See how far you can hit them and how much you can curve them without falling down. It's a great game to improve your tempo and balance.

217

If you're having trouble pinpointing where you need help, keeping statistics is a pretty good idea.

foot putt unless you can do it again. It's a wonderful training game, both for your shotmaking and your concentration.

Three-ball total. Take three balls out in the late afternoon or whenever the course isn't crowded and see what kind of total score you can make with them. Keep track of all your statistics. See how many fairways you hit, how many greens you hit in regulation, how many times you get it up and down with your recovery shots, how many putts you have.

If you're having trouble pinpointing where your game needs help, keeping statistics is a pretty good idea during an actual round. Over a period of time you'll be able to determine your strengths and weaknesses pretty well.

Games around the green. I've been called a left-brained player, more mechanical than creative, and to some extent that may be true. But I've always been very creative, with a very good touch, in the short-game area. That's because I learned to be creative around the greens by playing all the games Mr. Penick gave us when we were growing up. Crenshaw also is one of the most creative short-game players, and I'm sure it's for the same reason.

Playing these games not only will improve your physical skill but will give you more options, more chance to be creative when the occasion demands it on the course.

Pitching and chipping. Since the pitch shot is often just a longer version of the chip, most of these games apply to both areas and can be played interchangeably.

• Learn your distances. I seldom—almost never—work on my swing when I'm practicing my wedge play. I'm always trying to fly the ball different distances. You can go out and work on your swing and hit 40 wedge shots to a 70-yard target, and eventually you end up with a wonderful pattern of balls around that 70-yard flag. That's perfect provided you get a 70-yard wedge shot every time on the course. But it's not so good if you get a 30-yard shot and you haven't worked on that distance.

Instead, stake out targets at different distances—you can

HIT DRIVER FROM DIFFERENT TEE HEIGHTS
With your driver, hit the ball teed at different heights—very high, very low and on the ground. Swing smoothly. This will teach you to control the club.

use range buckets or ball-bags or clubs—and hit shots to them. Set the targets at 10-yard intervals from 20 yards to 80 or 90 yards. Try to fly the ball to the target without worrying about roll. That you can adjust on the course to hard or soft greens just by flying the ball closer to or farther from the hole. Go up and down the ladder, then skip around to different distances. Hit no more than three shots to each target. It's pretty easy after a few shots to develop a feel for the distance, but you don't get that many on the course.

After a few sessions you'll develop a feel for how much swing you need for each distance. Then when you get a 30-yard or a 50-yard shot on the course you'll say, gosh, I've hit this shot. I can handle it.

Go out on the course when there is no one around and hit pitch shots from different distances on different holes to get a feel for actual playing conditions. Be sure to repair your ball marks, of course.

• Play pitch shots from different slopes—uphill, downhill and sidehill—and watch how the ball reacts, how it comes off the club, how much it runs or how quickly it stops after it lands. Play them from bad lies, from hardpan and divots and especially from the rough.

• See how high you can hit a pitch shot. Find an object—a bush or a tree or stand your golf bag in front of you—and see how close you can get to it and still loft the ball over it.

• See if you can hit a low spinner and check it up quickly. You never know when you're going to have to play under a tree limb and over a bunker and still stop the ball in a hurry.

• Especially good for developing feel is the blind pitch. Find an elevated green and stand where you can't see the flag from the base of the slope. Walk up, look at the flag, then walk back and hit pitch shots, relying totally on feel to strike the ball the proper distance. Vary the distance to get a feel for shots of different lengths.

• Pitch a ball to the flag, then walk up and try to hole the putt. Do this each time. It's what you'll be doing on the course, so teach yourself to do it in practice. It makes each

You'll say, gosh, I've hit this shot. I can handle it.

HIT TO DIFFERENT TARGETS

Play the ball to different targets. In this case, chip to different holes on the practice green, no more than two or three shots at a time to each hole, to develop a feel for distance.

shot and each putt important, and it teaches you the discipline to finish the hole. A good pitch isn't worth much if you don't make the putt.

• As with the pitching clubs, you need to practice uphill, downhill and sidehill chip shots. Practice out of bad lies, particularly the collar of rough that you often find around the green. Practice the bellied wedge shot I described in the short-game chapter.

• See which club or clubs you can get closest with. From various distances, hit five or ten balls with almost every club in your bag and see what happens. See if you can get it closer with a pitching wedge or a 7-iron or a 5-iron. Usually you'll find that the longer the chip, the less-lofted club you'll want to use.

• Other than that, my rule for chipping practice is the same as for pitching. Never hit more than two or three balls in a row to any single target. And vary your targets, from short to long, being sure to skip around.

• Drop a bunch of balls on the fringe, with the flagstick 35 to 50 feet away. Land the first ball on the green as close to the edge as possible. Then chip each successive ball past the previous ball, leaving it as close to the previous ball as you can. Alter your aim a little to make sure you don't hit the previous ball. This game is more for your distance touch than accuracy. See how many balls you can chip between the fringe and the cup. Or you can do it the opposite way. Try to leave your first chip just short of the cup and each successive chip shorter than the next. This game teaches the all-important feel for distance.

That's also a good game for pitch shots from a little farther away.

• Try to land your chips on a particular spot. Put a ring the size of a hula hoop, or smaller as you get better, on the edge of the green where you want the ball to land. Outlining the area with several tees is probably the best way to do it. Then try to land your chips within that circle. You can do the same with pitches. Don't be concerned about how far the ball

A good pitch isn't worth much if you don't make the putt.

THE BLIND PITCH

Pitch to an elevated green from where you can't see the flag. Rely totally on feel to strike the ball the proper distance, and vary the distance to get a feel for shots of different lengths.

PITCH AND HOLE OUT

Pitch one ball at a time to the flag, then walk up and try to hole the putt. This teaches you to do what you'll be doing on the course, and it makes each shot and putt important.

Eventually you'll establish a feeling for where you must land the ball.

rolls. You're just trying to land on a target. Eventually, by playing all these games, you'll establish a feeling for where you must land the ball to make it roll a specific distance with a certain club. This game develops a feel for hitting that spot.

You can accomplish much the same thing by laying your umbrella on the green and chipping balls over it while still keeping them around the hole. Vary the spot where you place the umbrella. See how close to the hole you can put it and what club you need to still get the ball close.

• Play chip-in with a friend. Alternate shots, and the player who gets the closest to the hole gets one unit. If he chips it in, he gets five units. Play a match to see who gets the most units in a specified number of holes. The winner gets the prize, whether it's a beer or a dollar or whatever you want to play for. Again, that makes each chip shot important.

• By yourself, you can play the same chip-and-hole-out game you did with the pitch shots. Or, if you really want to make it tough on yourself at the end of your practice session, you can set a certain number of chips to hole before you let yourself go home. Tell yourself you have to hole three chips at three different holes before you go.

You might be late for dinner a few times, but you'll become a better chipper.

Bunker games. Many, if not most, amateurs who land in the sand are simply trying to get out, hopefully in one stroke. That's the first order of business, of course, but to become a good player and shoot the best score you can, you need to develop versatility in your bunker play to be able to get the ball reasonably close most of the time.

Once you become fairly proficient with the basic bunker shot, practice from the slopes—uphill, downhill and sidehill. Practice hitting balls from buried lies and from fried-egg lies.

Most of the games I've described also apply to bunker practice. Have some fun with them from all these situations.

• I particularly like the backup game from the bunker. Hit your first ball short of the target, then each successive ball shorter than the last and still get out of the bunker. See how

CHIP OVER AN UMBRELLA

Place your umbrella on the green and chip balls over it. Vary the placement of the umbrella and see how close you can get the ball to the hole with various clubs. This establishes a feel for where you have to land the ball with different clubs to get the shots close.

CHIP EACH BALL SHORTER

To learn a feel for distance, chip your first ball just short of your target, in this case your umbrella lying on the green. Then try to chip the next ball shorter than the previous one and see how many you can get between the target and the fringe. You can do the same with pitch shots from farther away.

Most players can hit sand shots in the right direction, but many have little feel for how far the ball will go.

many you can do in a row, or how many you can put between the fringe and your first ball. Most players can hit sand shots the right direction, but many have little feel for how far the ball will go. This game is excellent for developing that feel out of the sand.

It's also a wonderful competitive game, either by yourself or with a friend. Set a goal for yourself on how many successful shots you can hit. Or bet your buddy that you can do better than he.

• Practice trajectory and spin. See how high you can hit the ball out of the bunker and how quickly you can stop it. See how low you can hit it. See how much spin you can put on it. A variation of the umbrella game works here. Lay the umbrella short of the hole and see if you can land a high shot over the umbrella and still stop it around the target.

• Hit bunker shots with different clubs, with a 9-iron or 7-iron or 5-iron. See if you can hit a nice, soft, 20-yard blast with a 2-iron. Seve Ballesteros is a master at these shots. You may not have Seve's ability, but he had to learn sometime and so can you. Lay the clubface way open and find out what kind of swing you have to make to explode the ball out of the sand. The point is that if you learn to do this even halfway proficiently, shots with the sand wedge begin to look pretty easy.

• As the ultimate test, don't allow yourself to leave the bunker until you hole a certain number of shots. Gary Player says he used to stay there until he holed three shots. Sometimes it may have taken him four or five shots. Other times it might have taken him 1,000.

Set your own number, whether it's to hole one or hit the pin with one or whatever your expectations are. You might miss not only dinner but the late evening news a few times, but you'll get better out of the bunker.

Putting games. As I've said, there are two aspects to becoming successful on the greens. You have to develop a good stroke and you have to develop a touch, a feel for distance and break. The games and drills that follow will help you do both. Be sure to put them together, keeping in mind Mr. Penick's philosophy that the best stroke in the world isn't worth much without touch, and a less-than-classic stroke can work well if you have confidence in it and have good touch.

All practice can and should be fun, but putting practice can be the most fun of all. You can do it at your leisure. You can do it on your noon hour without getting sweaty. You can do it before a round and after a round. You can do it in the evening before or after dinner. You can do it by yourself or with friends. It's especially enjoyable with a group of buddies, putting around the clock for a few cents or a few dollars or whatever it is that stimulates your competitive instincts.

And if it helps you develop your skill on the green, which it will, you'll reap the biggest payoff of all when you get on the course.

So play these games. Set whatever standards or goals you want for them. There is no pass or fail here. You'll raise your standards as your skill increases. Learn and enjoy at the same time.

• Use a chalk line. You can buy a carpenter's chalk line at a hardware store and snap a straight line down on the green. Then try to hit short and medium-length putts along that line. That will develop a straight-back-and-through stroke, a good mechanical stroke, but it won't develop the touch you need to become a good putter. I see guys on Tour who hit putt after putt for hours down a chalk line. And that's wonderful, if they happen to get a straight-in putt on every hole. But it doesn't help them make a 30-foot breaking putt. They are perfecting a stroke, which is fine, but a perfect stroke does not always make a good putter.

• Make 100 three-foot putts in a row. Okay, you laugh, but it can be done and it's an effective game if you have trouble with short putts. Bobby Wadkins, who had a lot of problems with short putts, improved tremendously by doing this drill. Just start hitting three-footers and keep hitting them. Don't hit them from exactly the same spot, because eventually you would wear a trench in the green which would help the ball

All practice can be fun, but putting practice can be the most fun of all.

PLAY BACKUP FROM THE BUNKER
This game develops a feel for distance out of the sand. Select a target on the green and try to hit your first shot out of the bunker short of that target. Then try to put each successive ball short of the previous one.

HIT DIFFERENT CLUBS FROM THE BUNKER
Hit various clubs from the bunker, from a 9-iron on down to a 5-iron or 2-iron. Lay the clubface open and find out what kind of swing you have to make to explode the ball out softly. It will make the shot with the sand wedge look easy.

PUTT ALONG A CHALK LINE

Lay a chalk line along the ground and hit short and medium-length putts to develop a straight-back-and-through stroke. Be aware that this can develop a good stroke but not necessarily good touch.

go in and give you a false sense of security. Not only does this game develop your stroke, it develops your confidence. The sight of the ball going into the hole time after time will build your confidence. So when you face a three-footer on the golf course, it won't seem like such a big deal.

• Putt blindly. Hit three putts in succession without looking up at the target. Try to get the balls to end up as close together as possible simply by duplicating the feel of your stroke. This is a great game to identify and develop feel in your stroke.

• Putt looking at the hole. This is another good game to develop feel and free up the stroke. Line up the putterface, look at the hole and make the stroke without looking back at the ball. It's especially effective with short putts, and you'll be surprised at how many of them you make. It gets you out of the mechanical mode and into thinking about the target. I've putted this way in competition, most recently the 1990 Kemper Open, and have made a lot of putts doing it.

The same thing works with chipping, by the way.

Taking practice swings with your eyes shut is a similar way to develop a feel for your stroke.

• Putt from around the hole. Place ten balls around the hole, all at a given distance, and see how many you can make. In other words, don't just try to make ten six-footers in a row from the same spot. Hit ten different six-footers. Then vary the distance. Hit ten three-footers, 12-footers and 20-footers. Or vary the distance within each group around the hole. Keep track of how many you make from the different distances, then try to beat that mark. This is a game in which you can compete with yourself, and it's also great fun to do with a friend.

• Make putts from three, six and nine feet. This one puts a lot of pressure on you and teaches you how to handle it. Put three balls at three feet, three at six feet and three at nine feet. You have to hole all three at three feet before you go to the balls at six feet. You have to hole all of them before you go to nine feet. Then you have to hole all three from there. If

When you face a three-footer on the course, it won't seem like such a big deal.

MAKE 100 THREE-FOOTERS

Try to make 100 three-foot putts in a row, varying the spot slightly so you don't wear a trench in the green. This will develop a good short-putt stroke and will build your confidence on the short testers.

PUTT BLINDLY

Hit three putts in succession without looking up. Try to make the balls end up as close together as possible by duplicating the feel of your stroke. This will help you identify feel and develop touch.

The pressure builds with every putt, but it's no different than the pressure you face on the course.

you miss at any stage, you have to go back to the three-footers. The last few are tough, especially from the nine-foot range. The pressure builds with every putt, but it's no different than the pressure you face on the course, and this game instills the ability to handle that pressure.

• Play drawback. This is a wonderful game, especially when you're playing it competitively with a friend. Putt from various distances, and every time you miss a putt you must draw the ball back the length of your putter. So every time you miss you have to make at least a three-foot putt and probably one that is longer. This teaches you to make those difficult three- and four-foot putts when they count.

• Stroke to a target. Lag one ball to a particular point, 20 feet or more away. Then hit a ball to another point. Pick a target at any distance and try to get the ball as close as possible. This teaches you the amount of stroke you need to get the ball a certain distance.

• Practice breaking putts. Hit putts both short and long on slopes and watch how they react. It's the only way I know to learn to make them.

• Stroke long putts. No matter what other games you play that I've mentioned, and you should play them all, probably the most important aspect of your putting practice is to hit long putts. I'm talking very long—40, 50 and 60 feet or more. Do this more than you practice your short putts. You can sometimes stab a short putt into the hole with a short, jerky stroke and not know the difference. But a bad stroke on a long putt shows up every time when you miss the hole by ten feet or more. Hitting long putts will help you develop a stroke that will work from any distance.

See how close you can get the first putt from, say, 50 feet. Then try to get the next one closer, and the next one closer than that. Then choose a different target and do the same thing. Or compete with your buddy.

You also can get double benefit by watching how the long putts break and getting a feel for slopes. It's fun, and it's the best thing you can do for your putting.

PUTT FROM AROUND THE HOLE

Place ten balls around the hole and see how many you can make. First place all ten at a given distance, then vary the distance within the group.

MAKE PRESSURE PUTTS

Place three balls at three feet, three at six feet and three at nine feet. You have to make all three from each distance before you can move on. The pressure increases with each putt, and this teaches you to handle it.

PLAY DRAWBACK

Putt from various distances, and each time you miss pull the ball back a putter-length farther away than where it stops. This helps you face the difficult short putts on the course.

PUTT LOOKING AT THE HOLE

Line up the putter, look at the hole and putt without looking back at the ball. This gets you out of the mechanical mode, frees up your stroke and gets you thinking about the target.

Those are the games I recommend for your practice sessions. And I'll bet you can come up with others. Do so, because the more fun you have in practice, the more you enjoy it, the better you're going to prepare yourself to make a good score on the course.

THE PREPARATION BEFORE YOU PLAY Practicing and warming up are often confused, or considered the same, which they are not. In the former, you're trying to learn how to play. In the latter, you're preparing to play.

Unfortunately, the warmup session is one of the most-neglected factors in playing golf, at least as far as amateurs are concerned. Professionals take a great deal of care in warming up, but an amateur with a 9 o'clock tee time is likely to arrive at the course at 8:45, jerk on his shoes and take only a couple of hurried practice swings before he tees it up.

In most other sports, individual or team, there's some time built in for warming up, and the participants do it as a matter of course. But in golf, which may be the most difficult game in the world to play from the standpoint of hand, eye and muscular coordination, players tend to rush out and start cold turkey. Then they wonder why they go five over par on the first three holes and ruin the round before they really get started.

So the first step in preparing for a round of golf is giving yourself time to prepare. The next step is doing it correctly.

The warmup session is really not that at all. It's a preparation session. If you want to warm up, to loosen your muscles, sit down and do some stretching exercises. That's a much better way of getting your muscles loose. Then start really warming up or preparing for golf.

That real warmup or preparation session is to set the tone for the day. It has to do with the mental outlook. It involves going through the routine and working on the shots that you're going to use on the golf course.

In my case, I'll usually go first to the putting green, drop

The more fun you have in practice, the better you prepare yourself to make a good score.

three balls and just hit a few putts. I'm really trying to make them. I'm not just working on my stroke.

After that I'll go to the practice tee. Before a round I'll hit my even-numbered clubs. After a round I'll practice with the odd clubs. That just happens to be my routine. You may not be into post-round practice as the professionals are, but during your week of golf you should try to practice with every club in your bag.

I may hit eight or ten balls with each club. For the first few balls I'll be paying close attention to my routine and tempo. On the last two swings with each club I warm up with I'll focus in on hitting shots—a high cut or a hook or a really low shot into the wind. Then I'll go to the next club and do the same thing. With the last two swings with each club I'll be playing a particular golf shot, the way I would on the golf course. I'm not working on my swing. I'm not thinking about mechanics. I'm playing golf. I'm preparing myself to concentrate on playing before I ever set foot on the first tee.

I'll do the same thing with the short game. I'll play some bunker shots and chip shots as if they count.

Finally, I'll go back to the putting green, this time with only one ball. I'm into the tempo and routine of swinging the club and hitting shots, and now I'm trying to make putts with that one ball. If I miss, I can't shrug it off and drag another one over and say, well, two out of three isn't bad. I'm playing golf.

So when I get on the first tee I'm not unsure of myself. I've already hit drives that counted on the practice tee. I've already hit iron shots and chip shots and bunker shots and putts that counted. So whatever I encounter on the first hole and the holes thereafter, it won't be the first time I've hit that shot that day. I've already practiced making it count.

Have fun practicing and learning how to play. Prepare properly each time before you play. Then have more fun watching your scores go down.

The warmup or preparation session is to set the tone for the day.

CHAPTER 7/ MANAGING YOUR GAME

One of the most important factors in playing consistently good golf is the ability to manage your game.

The victories started to come more regularly after 1981. For the rest of the '80s and into 1990 I won at least one tournament every year except 1988.

In 1982, at the Bay Hill Classic, I shot 69 in the final round to overtake Jack Nicklaus and Denis Watson. Then I made that chip on the first extra hole to win. That was my only victory of the year, but I did win my second straight Vardon Trophy with a 70.21 scoring average and finished third on the money list.

The next year I shot my record 62 at Pebble Beach in the third round of the Crosby, then finished with 73 in the rain on Sunday to win by two strokes.

I finished ninth on the money list that year. Except for 1985, when I fell to 14th, that was the worst I was going to be for the rest of the decade. Consistency was starting to pay off.

The ability to play consistently good golf comes from many factors, as I've explained. One of those factors, and one of the most important, is the ability to manage your game on the course. You can call it strategy or whatever you want, but in the end it comes down to playing smart golf. I've always prided myself on my ability to do that, and I'm convinced that everybody, no matter what handicap level, can improve his or her score by doing the same.

To play golf intelligently, to best manage your game through an 18-hole round, you have to know two things— you have to know what you can do and you have to be aware of what the architect wants you to do.

Figure out the design. Architects are very deceptive in the way they design golf courses. I know, because I'm involved in course design, and I can assure you that the course architect wears different shoes than the golfer. The object of any good designer is to make the course fair for all golfers, whatever their skill levels, but to offer a risk versus reward challenge to the better player. . . or to anybody who wants to accept the challenge. They want you to try to make a good score with the proviso that if you don't, you risk making a much higher score. In other words, they want you to try to make a 4, knowing that if you played safe you could make a 5 all week long and in trying to make that 4 you sometimes may come up with a 6 or 7.

Years ago we used to play our Orlando tournament at Rio Pinar, which has a par-5, dogleg right with a bunch of tremendously tall pine trees at the corner. Everybody hit his drive as close to the right side as possible because it shortened the hole. It was impossible for most of us to cut the corner over those trees, but if you could do that and hit it into the adjacent fairway, you could hit as little as a 6- or 7-iron into the green. You were just taking the hypotenuse of the right triangle. At the time, Bobby Mitchell was one of the better players on Tour and was notorious for taking any gamble he could. I remember one tournament at Rio Pinar in which he tried to cut that dogleg every time. I don't remember his exact scores, but I think he made two 3s, a 4 and a 9. That still put him one under par on the hole for the

The course architect wears different shoes than the golfer.

tournament, but by playing it safe he possibly could have been two or three under.

That's why the architect gives you choices. You pay your money and you take your chances.

In the early days of golf most courses were *penal* in nature, because that was the philosophy then and probably because they were laid out more by nature than by man. There were bunkers and, in some cases, water that crossed in front of the driving area and in front of the green. The player had to either carry a long shot over these hazards or lay up, probably sacrificing a stroke, and carry a shorter shot over them. There was no other way to get to the green, so you almost always were penalized severely for a bad shot.

Nowadays the designers are building more *strategic* courses that offer a number of options, several different ways to play the hole. For instance, there are more doglegs being built, because they offer so many different ways to play the hole. Strategic courses make you figure out the best route to the hole within your capabilities.

A combination of those two philosophies is the *heroic* concept, popularized by Robert Trent Jones. This design offers the best of both worlds, a chance to gamble for the player who wants to, and a safe way for the player who can't. Bunkers and water hazards are placed in a position that will entice you to play across them to save a stroke or possibly two. But if you miss, the penalty is severe. If you don't want to make that gamble or if your ability doesn't allow you to make the carry, there are safer routes that will let you skirt the hazard and still have a chance to pitch and putt for your par. Jones's philosophy is to provide for an easy bogey but a difficult par, and an even more difficult birdie. Many architects have since incorporated that concept into their designs.

Beware when you play a course. Architects are sneaky. They purposely lure you in the direction of trouble, and they entice you into thinking you can make it over that trouble. And maybe you can. But before you try it you should evaluate the safer route that any good designer will give you.

Beware when you play a course. Architects are sneaky.

Play to your strengths. The key to playing any golf course strategically, as with any other endeavor, is to play to your strengths and away from your weaknesses. A person who is a good course manager is consistently able to find a way to hit the shot that he hits best.

For example, in the U.S. Open at Winged Foot in 1959, Ben Hogan figured out how he wanted to play the sixth hole, a 324-yard par 4 to a smallish, L-shaped green with a deep bunker at the front right and water left and behind. Most of the pros were playing it with a 2-iron and a wedge, but Hogan decided he wanted a longer second shot so he could spin it more and hold it on the green. So he paced off 150 yards from the middle of the green back toward the tee, then walked from that point back to the tee. That was another 175 yards, so Hogan played a 5-iron from the tee and had a full 7-iron into the green.

When Billy Casper won that same Open, he is supposed to have laid up every round on the third hole, a par 3 that plays well longer than 200 yards and has a narrow, sloping green that is guarded by deep bunkers left and right. Getting up and down from those bunkers is risky, at best, so Casper figured he had a better chance at par every day by playing short. And he made par every day.

He did much the same thing when he won the Masters in 1970. He made up his mind before the tournament started that he was going to lay up on all the par-5 holes. He figured he was a good wedge player and a good putter and had a good chance to get his birdies that way. So he made no effort to go for any of them in two. That took a lot of pressure off his tee shots, because he didn't feel he had to crunch them out there, or cut the dogleg on the 13th. So his tee shots became better, he put his second shots right where he wanted them for the best shots at the flags. He played the par 5s well under par and he won the tournament.

Casper felt that his strengths were his wedge play and his putting, not his driving or fairway wood play, so he didn't try to force those. Hogan felt his strength on that one hole was a

A good course manager is consistently able to find a way to hit the shot that he hits best.

An individual's strengths determine how he plays most golf courses.

full 7-iron, not a short wedge, so that's the way he played it.

In my case, I'm an excellent wedge player, one of the best on Tour right now, so I'll find ways to put myself in positions where I can hit that wedge. Take a short par 4 with a lot of trouble on it, where most players are hitting long irons off the tee and leaving themselves with 7- or 8-iron second shot. If I can hit a driver off the tee and get myself into wedge range, I may attack that hole.

The fourth at Pebble Beach is a perfect example. It's only 325 yards, up a hill, but the Pacific Ocean borders the right side of the fairway and deep bunkers are on the left. Most players hit a 1-iron or 4-wood off the tee and leave them-selves a full pitching wedge or 9-iron for the second shot. On the other hand, I will always hit at least a 3-wood, and half the time I'll hit the driver. That puts me where I have a sand wedge or a 60-degree wedge left. If I get those clubs in my hand, I'm in good shape, so I'll tend to play that hole very aggressively.

Of course, it also helps that I'm a pretty straight driver, but there is still some risk there. You just have to weigh that risk against the potential reward.

In just about every case I can think of on Tour, an individual's strengths determine how he plays most golf courses. Mark Calcavecchia, for example, is an excellent chipper and an outstanding player with all the little wedge shots around the green. And he has the imagination and confidence to play them successfully. He's among the best on Tour right now from close-in around the green. So it doesn't bother him to miss greens, because he plays those shots so well that he knows he can recover. Consequently he can shoot at a lot of pins that a lesser short-game player wouldn't go for.

Greg Norman is another good example. He's the best bunker player on Tour today. He learned a lot from Seve Ballesteros, who also is outstanding from the bunkers. So Norman, like Calcavecchia, can fire at the flags and not worry if he ends up in a bunker. He can get it up and down.

That's one reason—I'm sure personality is another—Mark

and Greg are easily the most explosive players on Tour. They have the strength to actually overpower a golf course, which few players do. Most of us move the chess men all around the board and eventually end up defeating the opponent. Calcavecchia and Norman have the ability to come in and just turn the table upside down. But they couldn't and wouldn't do it without great short games.

Curtis Strange is the best driver on Tour. He's not nearly the longest, but he puts the ball where he wants to more times than most. He puts it in position where he has the best opportunity to take advantage of the hole. That's why he doesn't make many mistakes. That's why he plays the difficult courses well. That's why he's won two U.S. Opens.

I'd pick John Mahaffey as the best fairway wood player out here. He's very straight, he has tremendous control over the height he wants to hit the ball and he can work the ball in both directions. John isn't long off the tee, but he can overcome that with his fairway wood play. He can do some things on the longer holes that other players might not be able to. The fairway woods are his strength, and he uses it well.

Bruce Lietzke is the best long-iron player. He hits the long irons very high and with a natural fade, so the ball comes down softly. That's very hard to do with a long iron and still make the ball go the distance you want. But Bruce can use his long irons both from the tee on tight holes and for shots into a tucked pin that other players can't make.

In my opinion, by the way, Lietzke is about the best player we have from the standpoint of the total game. He can leave the rest of us behind. I think it's fabulous for the rest of the Tour that he likes to take time off to race cars and go fishing.

Paul Azinger is probably the best middle-iron player. David Frost may be our best short-iron player. He has a wonderful ability to control his trajectory and then the distance. So both of these players, I'm sure, try to set up situations where they are hitting their best clubs as often as possible.

The best putter on Tour right now is Steve Jones. He

I think it's fabulous for the rest of the Tour that Lietzke likes to race cars and go fishing.

DAVID FROST
Control of distance and trajectory makes him skilled at short-iron play.

GREG NORMAN
His skill out of the bunker lets him be aggressive in attacking the hole.

JOHN MAHAFFEY
Fairway wood play helps him overcome lack of length off the tee.

CURTIS STRANGE
He's the best driver, because he puts it where he can best take advantage of the hole.

246

PAUL AZINGER
He positions for the middle-iron shot, at which he may be the best.

STEVE JONES
Skill with the putter takes the pressure off the rest of his game.

BRUCE LIETZKE
His ability to hit high, soft long-iron shots lets him do things others can't.

MARK CALCAVECCHIA
He's a magician around the green, so he can be aggressive.

hasn't been around long enough to prove his longevity, but he has a wonderfully simple and effective putting stroke. Mark O'Meara is a great putter. So is Calcavecchia . . . and Ben Crenshaw, of course. What putting ability does, of course, is give you a lot of flexibility with your on-course strategy. I don't know how each of these individuals approaches it, but basically a good putter can gamble a little and feel he can save par with a putt if the gamble doesn't work. Or he does *not* have to gamble trying to get close to a hidden pin or with a tricky shot out of a bunker. He doesn't have to lay every shot stiff, because he feels he can make some longer putts. This takes a lot of pressure off.

The point is, I'm sure that if you would discuss it with any of the players I've mentioned, or almost everybody else on Tour, they go around the course trying to set up situations in which they can play their strongest suit.

You should do the same. You know what your strengths are on the golf course, which shots you play well and which you play poorly. Practice to improve your weaknesses, because that will improve your range of options and eventually make you a better player. In the meantime, go with your best shot.

Golf is a chess game. So much of golf is having been there and knowing what's going to happen if you try something. It's being able to plan ahead. In everything else that people do, in any type of business, they can plan ahead because they're aware of what they're doing. They've been there before. Maybe they haven't seen the exact situation, but they've seen something very similar. So based on their experiences, based on their knowledge of their abilities, they're able to decide on a particular option.

Golf is no different. If you haven't been there. If you haven't failed a few times—probably a bunch of times—and succeeded a few times, there is no way you can know what's going to happen.

The more times you've been there, the more data you

> They go around the course trying to set up situations in which they can play their strongest suit.

have in your computer . . . as long as you put it in your computer. You have to take advantage of whatever experience you've had. And that's a problem with a lot of players. They really don't pay attention to what happens during a round of golf. The data is there, but they don't enter it into the computer. So that data is not available to them the next time they face a similar situation.

It's like playing chess. If you've played chess for a while and have paid attention, you can anticipate what's going to happen. You don't just move a knight without anticipating some move four, five or even ten moves down the line.

In golf, you don't pull a club out of the bag without anticipating that it's going to get you into a position where you have a good chance to hit another effective shot.

For example, a 70-yard shot into the green is a very good distance for me. I'll land the ball closer to the pin, time after time, from 70 yards than I will from 30 or 40 yards. That's because a 70-yard shot is a full swing for me with the 60-degree wedge, and it's much easier to hit a full shot the correct distance than it is a partial shot. You have so many variables with a partial shot—how to slow down your swing, how to shorten your swing—that it's difficult to hit the shot the required distance consistently.

It's the same with any club. If you give a player a full shot at a distance he feels comfortable with, he has a pretty good chance of hitting it the correct distance. The professional will and even the high handicapper will if he makes the right swing.

So 70 yards is a good distance for me with the wedge. If I'm playing a par-5 hole that I can't reach in two, I will do my best to put my second shot 70 yards from the hole. I figure out the total distance I have to the hole and subtract the 70 yards. That's how far I want to play my second shot.

It has worked pretty well. One year at Augusta it seemed like every time I tried to get to 70 yards, I never missed it by more than a couple of yards. And when you're trying to do something and accomplish it, you feel great. Not only has

Get into a position where you have a good chance to hit another effective shot.

Being 100 yards away is better than being in the bunker. So make sure you don't get in the bunker.

your course management been perfect and you feel good about the shot coming up, you also just hit a perfect shot, which boosts your confidence even more. So everything is set for the third shot to be a great one.

So, assess your strengths and decide on that basis how you're going to play the hole. If you think you can't get to a par-5 hole in two, don't just blast your second shot somewhere up around the green. Figure out where you want to be. Maybe your best play to the green is from 50 yards. Your next best play is from 100 yards. Your third best play is from the greenside bunker. Well, don't hit the 3-wood thinking you just might get on the green and wind up in the greenside bunker instead. Being 50 yards back is better than being in the bunker. Being 100 yards away is better than being in the bunker. So make sure you don't get in the bunker.

I play a game in my mind called "backpedaling." It's essentially the same thing Hogan was doing physically when he paced off the sixth hole at Winged Foot from the green back. I start from the green and go back to the tee and decide where I want every shot to be. That means I have to decide where I want to put the previous shot.

For example, if the green is sloping and fast, it's advantageous to keep the ball below the hole so you have an uphill putt. Or if it slopes right to left, you may want to aim the ball a little left of the pin to get that same straight uphill putt and give yourself the best opportunity to make it.

Now I have to figure out the best place from which to play my shot to the green so I can get the ball where I want it on the putting surface. If it's a par-4 hole, that's where I want to hit my drive. If it's a par 5, that's where I want my second shot to wind up, and I'll have to decide where I want to put my tee shot so I'll have the best chance to get the second shot in position.

All the while I'm taking into consideration my strengths and avoiding my weaknesses. I may want to hit a 3-iron off the tee because that leaves me with XYZ yardage, and I'm really good from that yardage. I don't want to hit a driver off

250

the tee because I'm not so good at ZYX yardage and that's what a driver would leave me.

Back to that chess game. I'm sure the masters are able to start with the move to checkmate, go back to check, go back through all the moves that would lead up to that and ultimately end up at the opening, moving the pawn ahead two squares.

It helps a lot if you know the golf course, and you certainly should know your own course and any others you've played a time or two. Even if this is your first time around, you can figure out a lot of these things simply by looking at the hole, seeing where the hazards are, noting the slope of the green and the pin position and checking the yardage.

Figure out, if you can, how the architect is trying to deceive you. Then beat him at his own game.

Love all your clubs. Successful course management is a lot easier if you are proficient with all the clubs in your bag. That starts with improving your technique in practice. It finishes with having trust in all your clubs.

When somebody asks me what my favorite clubs are, I say that I have 14 of them. I'd better have 14, because sooner or later I'm going to encounter a situation where I have to hit a particular club. If I hate that club, then I have to work around it. Or I can't hit it when I need to. I don't ever want to be in that position. Never have a club in your bag that you shy away from.

By the same token, you don't want a favorite club, because that means the rest of them are less your favorites.

Yet so many amateurs I play with violate this philosophy. They love the 8-iron, but they hate the 2-iron. Part of that may be a swing problem, but often it's psychological. If you like your 8-iron, you should like your 7-iron. If you like your 7, you should like your 6-iron. If you like your 6, you should like your 5, and so on down through the set.

You may like all the clubs through the set until you get to the 3-iron. You can't hit your 3-iron, but you love your 2-

Never have a
club in your
bag that you
shy away from.

It's basically a matter of weighing the reward against the risk.

iron. That means you don't have a swing problem. You probably have a bad 3-iron. And that happens more than most amateurs realize. Sets that are supposed to be perfectly matched often aren't.

So get rid of your 3-iron, or get it adjusted so it feels like the rest of your clubs. There is no point in carrying a club you can't hit or you're afraid to hit, because you're never going to hit a good shot with it.

If you love your 8-iron, my first recommendation is to make all your clubs feel like the 8-iron. Do whatever you have to do. Make sure they are all have the same balance, the proper weighting, the correct loft and lie. Ask your professional or a good clubmaker to help you.

Then swing all your clubs like you swing your 8-iron. That may be the best piece of advice I can give you.

When you should gamble. There are no clear-cut guidelines on when to gamble and when to play safe. It's basically a matter of weighing the reward against the risk—how great is the reward and how little is the risk. You have to consider both ends of the spectrum. If you gamble and pull it off, you can make a birdie or a par. If the shot doesn't work, are you going to make a bogey or is there a possibility of making a big number on the hole? Ask yourself, what is the least I can make and what is the most I can make? And is it worth it?

It would be nice if your options were always clear, but they seldom are. A lot depends on the situation. If you're in match play and your opponent is dormie and in good shape on the hole, you might as well go for it. You have nothing to lose. You have to win the rest of the holes anyway. But if the match is even and your opponent is down the middle, don't do anything foolish. He can miss a shot, too, before he finishes the hole. Or if you're in stroke play and are in or close to the lead, the risk might outweigh the reward. Maybe you should play it safe and try to make up a stroke somewhere else.

So much also depends on your skill level, and you have to

be realistic about that. Al Geiberger once told me about a situation he faced at Harbour Town during the Heritage Classic. He had driven his ball deep into the left woods, and as he walked up to it the marshal standing guard said, "You're dead." There was apparently no way to advance the ball toward the hole, but Al looked around and spotted a little hole in the trees that would let him get the ball back in play. He figured he could get an 8-iron through that hole, and he knocked his ball through the hole to within 20 yards of the green. He said the marshal was shaking his head as he walked away.

Granted, that may have been a low-percentage shot for Al Geiberger. Chances are it would certainly be a low-percentage shot for you. Consider a shot like that, but be realistic in making your decision. Don't delude yourself into thinking you can pull off a miracle shot if you've never come close to hitting such a shot before in your life. Utilize your strengths and never, ever, attempt a shot you can't play or that the circumstances won't let you play. Miracles come along only about every millennium or so.

Keep it in the fairway. When I first came on Tour I was not a long hitter, so I had to concentrate on being accurate. I'm a lot longer off the tee now, but at my size I'll never be a boomer, so I still have to be accurate.

It's easier to play golf from the fairway. Even on a fairly wide-open course, you still have a little rough, and you can't control the ball as well out of the rough. So you need to find a way to hit as many fairways as possible, no matter how long you hit it.

You can weigh length versus accuracy just like risk versus reward. It amounts to the same thing. If you can hit the tee shot 30 yards farther and miss one more fairway a round, then go for the 30 yards. The advantage of being two or three clubs closer on every hole is worth having to hit one more shot out of the rough. If you can hit it 20 yards farther and only miss one more fairway per round, you probably want to

Miracles come along only about every millennium or so.

go for the extra 20 yards. If you hit it only 10 yards farther and miss that one more fairway, you may be reaching the point where it's not worth it. If you get only five more yards with your best effort and it costs you one fairway per round, it's definitely not worth it. Or if you can hit it 30 yards farther but miss four more fairways a round, it's not worth it.

At some point in that equation you have to throttle back, or take a 3-wood or a long iron. No matter how far you hit the ball, if you're playing out of the rough all of the time you're going to have problems.

A lot of it depends on your skill level and particularly your strength factor. If you're a long hitter like Mark Calcavecchia and you can't hit enough fairways with the driver to play well, then you don't want or need to hit the driver as often as most players. Calcavecchia can hit his 3-wood or a long iron almost as far as I can hit my driver, so he's not giving up that much. If I don't hit my driver, I'm putting myself quite a way from the hole, so I have to use the driver more often. But I have to concentrate on hitting it straight or it doesn't do me any good.

No matter how far you hit the ball, if you're playing out of the rough all of the time you're going to have problems.

Another factor is the course you're playing. We play some courses that are fairly wide open. Torrey Pines in San Diego is an example. It's a public course with not much rough, and the winners there in recent years have been fairly long hitters. They just go ahead and bomb it long and aren't penalized much by the rough. But the guys who win at Pebble Beach or Riviera or Doral or Bay Hill or The Players Club are the one's who hit the fairways. They've had a good week of driving the ball. They may have driven it long, but above all they drove it straight.

Long is great, and you have to have a certain amount of length. You can't hit a 5-iron off the tee all the time. But straight is what produces good scores. Even if it costs you some distance, keep the ball in play.

Know your shot pattern. A common piece of advice I hear being given to amateurs is to take one more club than they think they need from a certain distance. I have a real problem with that, because basically you're telling them to allow for a miss, and that's not a very positive thought.

It's true that amateurs often fail to get the ball up to the pin. One reason is that they don't really understand how the pattern of their shots should relate to the target. Another is that they don't realistically know how far they hit each club on a consistent basis.

If you were to plot the typical amateur's shot pattern to a green, you'd find the center of that pattern is short of the pin. Draw a circle around all his shots to the green—left, right, long and short. Find the center of the pattern and invariably you'll find that point will be short of the pin.

The shot pattern for a professional or top amateur, on the other hand, will be basically a circle around the pin, with the center of his pattern near the cup. There will be as many shots long as there are short, as many right as left.

Charting shot patterns, whether they are yours or a Tour player's, can be very revealing, especially from the standpoint of showing what you're doing with your shots and what your expectations should be.

A professional's shot pattern with a long iron actually will be elliptical on the horizontal axis. He will hit more shots right and left than he will long and short. He can hit the club about the proper distance, but because it is a long iron he will hit more shots off line. But the center of his pattern still will be near the hole.

When I was deciding whether to put a 60-degree wedge in my bag, I charted every iron in my bag. My long-iron pattern was an ellipse, but as the club got shorter the pattern got rounder and rounder. When I got to the 8-iron I had almost a perfect circle around the target.

When I got to shots from 70 yards and less, which would call for the 60-degree wedge, I found that the pattern became elliptical again, but this time it was very narrow on the horizontal axis and longer on the vertical axis. There were partial shots that I could hit very straight but with more deviation in

The center of the typical amateur's shot pattern is short of the pin.

255

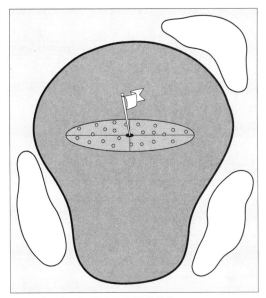

KITE'S LONG-IRON PATTERN

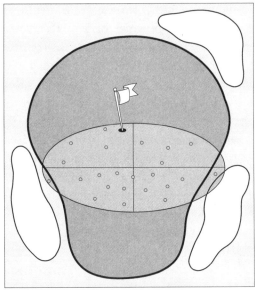

AMATEUR'S LONG-IRON PATTERN

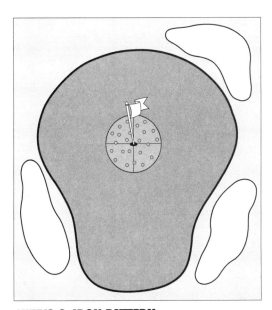

KITE'S 8-IRON PATTERN

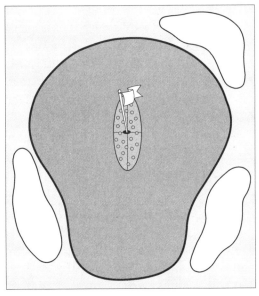

KITE'S PARTIAL-SHOT PATTERN

distance, because it's harder to hit those shots exactly as far as you want. But the center of the pattern was at the hole.

The problem with most amateurs is not that they can't get a particular club to the target, it's that they can't get the center of their pattern to the target. They can't hit the ball to the hole with that club on a consistent basis.

In pro-ams I'll pay attention to what my amateur partners do on the first couple of holes, and if it's obvious that they tend to underclub, I may give them extra yardage. I'll tell them the shot is longer than it actually is. In the rare cases where they overclub, I may give them less yardage. It's only when they show me that they can pull the right club out of the bag that I'll give them the proper yardage.

You once may have absolutely nailed a 7-iron 150 yards under certain conditions. So of course you can reach the hole with a 7-iron from 150 yards away. But don't make the mistake of assuming you can do it every time. Don't play for your absolute best on every shot. Instead, find out what your average is, what your pattern is. As I said in the chapter on practice, find out how far you carry each club. You may discover that your maximum length with a 7-iron may be 150 yards, but your average will be closer to 140.

And while you're at it, find out how far you *carry* your fairway woods and your driver. The knowledge could come in handy when you're playing over water or sand.

I suppose that, in effect, I'm telling you to use more club. But what I'm actually saying is use more common sense. Be realistic. Move the center of your pattern ahead to the hole. Somehow I think you'll score better.

Manage the weather. We all play golf at times under conditions that are not ideal. Sometimes it's cold. Some people choose to play in the cold. If you play winter golf, I'm sure you know how to dress for it and keep your hands and head warm. We on the PGA Tour often have to play in the rain. Even if you rarely choose to, it might rain during your club championship or member-guest and you could be forced to.

> Don't play for your absolute best on every shot. Find out what your average is.

Be prepared to cope with adverse conditions, both physically and mentally. In the first place, pack your golf bag properly. Have plenty of golf balls, enough gloves so that you can switch regularly during a rainy round, a rain suit, and umbrella, a bag cover or other cover to keep your clubs dry in the rain, a sweater, tape and bandages, a sunscreen lotion, everything you might need for all possible situations.

In the rain, you have to keep the grips on your clubs dry, your hands dry and your glove as dry as possible. When it gets so wet your hands are starting to slip during the swing, switch to a dry glove.

My problems are compounded by the fact that I wear glasses. I pull my visor or hat down to keep the rain off as much as possible. Beyond that, I just make up my mind that I'm going to have to wipe my glasses, just as I'm going to have to keep everything else dry.

If you have a choice and are physically capable, it's always better to walk with a caddie in the rain than ride a cart. The caddie can hold your umbrella and keep your equipment dry without your having to worry about it. On a cart, especially one with no windshield, the wind keeps whipping the rain into your face, there is no way to hold an umbrella and your clubs, sooner or later, get soaked.

The secret to playing well in the rain is to keep your composure. I make up my mind to play well and simply make coping with the rain part of my routine. That's why I feel very confident when playing in the rain. I don't like it any more than you do, but I try to take advantage of it.

This attitude helped me a lot during the final round of the 1983 Crosby. I had shot that record 62 in the third round and had the lead going into Sunday's play. It had rained the entire night before and rained during most of the final round. I shot 73, and while that doesn't sound very good, nobody else was doing much better under the conditions, and I ended up with a two-stroke victory.

Realize that if you can handle the problem better than anybody else, you're likely to win. The conditions are tough

> The secret to playing well in the rain is to keep your composure.

for everybody, and you have to believe that a lot of your fellow competitors will be distracted and complaining about the conditions instead of concentrating on their games.

With the right mental attitude under adverse conditions you can make a decent score, which will let you pass a lot of players.

Use common sense. Effective course management really boils down to a matter of common sense. When we let our expectations exceed our capabilities, we run into trouble. I've discussed assessing your strengths and weaknesses and planning your play accordingly, and that's really what golf is all about. The consideration is not *how* you make a score. It's what score you make and how high or low it is. If we all would take into account what we can and can't do, and consider the percentages, we all would score lower.

What I'm about to tell you really amounts to no more than using your head, but you'd be surprised how many golfers don't do that on the course.

Play away from trouble. I grew up in golf learning to play away from trouble, because my dad harped on that all the time. Never aim for trouble or curve a shot toward trouble. If there's a hazard on the left side of the fairway, tee the ball on the left side of the tee and hit your drive away from that hazard. If the trouble is on the right, tee it on the right and aim away from the potential problem.

Know where to miss it. This is a corollary to playing away from trouble. I'm not telling you to play for a missed shot, but that does happen sometimes, and if it does you want to miss it into the least dangerous situation.

On the 18th hole at Harbour Town, in the last round of the 1989 Nabisco Championships, I needed a par four to get into a playoff with Payne Stewart. I had a second shot of 190 yards into the green. The wind was blowing from right to left, and there's a marsh and other bad stuff on the left side. I aimed a 4-iron at the right side, hoping the wind would carry it onto the green. I sure wasn't going to miss the shot left.

The consideration is not *how* you make a score. It's what score you make.

The wind didn't take it enough, but the ball ended up just to the right of the green and I had a relatively simple 45-foot chip to the hole. I hit it to within three or three and a half feet and made the putt for the playoff and, eventually, the victory.

Be aware of where the trouble is, and play away from it.

Use your head in escaping trouble. As I discussed in Chapter 5, your first consideration in getting out of trouble is to get out. Then worry about getting to the green. Consider your lie, whether you have a shot and whether you have a swing, then decide on the shot you want to play. But consider your options, as Al Geiberger did at Harbour Town. There may be a better way than is readily apparent.

One year at Augusta, Hubert Green buried his second shot near the top lip of the bunker behind the seventh green. It looked like his only shot was to play away from the hole and end up with a 60-foot putt, which is never a bargain on those greens. But he took a 6-iron and chopped down on top of the ball, trying to run it out of the bunker. He knew if he rolled it out of the bunker he would be in good shape, and if he didn't he would have a good lie for a relatively easy second bunker shot. Well, the ball caught the lip and rolled back into the bunker, but he got it up and down for a bogey, which was absolutely the best he could have hoped for under the circumstances.

Mark Hayes won the Tournament Players Championship at Sawgrass in 1977 with the same kind of shot, only he got it out of the bunker and salvaged his par.

I had a similar situation on the 18th at Augusta one year. I had knocked my second shot into the top of the greenside bunker on the right. I wasn't buried, but the pin was on the top right and I had a long expanse of sand to carry and not much green to shoot at. I really didn't feel I could hit it hard enough and put enough spin on the ball to keep it on the green, so I took a 6-iron and ran it through the bunker. I was just playing for bogey, but the ball caught the lip perfectly and ended up about 10 feet from the hole. I made it for par,

There may be a better way than is readily apparent.

one of the best up and downs I've ever had.

So don't be foolish about it, but consider every opportunity. Every once in a while it can pay off.

Consider the conditions. Be aware that just because you can hit a particular club a certain number of yards on the practice tee, that might not be the yardage you always get on the course. You have to take into account whether the shot is uphill or downhill, whether the course is dry or wet, whether the air is heavy or light and how the wind is blowing. Consider the wind. It's usually difficult to determine exactly how hard the wind is blowing, or will be blowing at the precise moment you hit your shot, but you usually can make an educated guess. Experience plays a big part in helping you adjust your club selection in the wind.

Play the percentages. I've discussed assessing your strengths and weaknesses. Be realistic about this. Your capabilities, your skills, determine whether your chances of pulling off a shot are low or high.

If you have to strain to reach a par-5 hole, especially if it's over water or sand, lay up and play your best shot into the green.

If you're not a pinpoint iron player, don't aim for a pin that's tucked behind trouble. Aim for the fat part of the green and fade it or draw it into the pin. If the fade or draw doesn't come off, at the very least you'll be in the middle of the green. If you're not skilled at fading or drawing the ball on demand, just aim for the fat of the green anyway and take a chance on making a long putt. You at least have a good two-putt for par.

Don't try the shots you can't make consistently.

Effective course strategy is simply a matter of using your mind effectively. You do it all the time in your daily affairs. Do it on the golf course, too.

> Your skills determine whether your chances of pulling off a shot are high or low.

261

CHAPTER 8/
MANAGING
YOUR MIND

Basically, I wasn't having any fun.

Early in the 1984 season, during the Florida campaign, I met a man who has helped my career a lot. I had not had a very good west coast swing and had played horribly at the Honda Classic. I tied for 61st at 295, although I had just seen Peter Kostis before the tournament and he had told me my swing was good. I had hit the ball well, but I was not thinking patiently and was expecting the breaks to be all bad. Basically, I wasn't having any fun.

Peter was having trouble understanding why some of his students on Tour might not be playing well even though they were swinging well. So on Monday after the tournament he invited a group of us down to Boca Raton and introduced us to Dr. Bob Rotella, a sports psychologist at the University of Virginia. We sat down in a conference room and had a group discussion that lasted all morning, through lunch and into the early afternoon.

Doc told us a lot of things that we all knew and had used often but may have forgotten. I know I had. Just as it's difficult to keep your swing grooved all the time, it's difficult to keep your mind grooved. And that's just important as the physical part. Maybe more so.

Doc told us, "You have to have fun, you have to be easy on yourself, you have to focus on the good things and you have to be creative." He asked us when the last time was that we'd actually tried to play different shots, and I, for one, couldn't remember. I hadn't tried to hit a high cut or a low punch or any different shot in a number of weeks. I had been trying to make the perfect golf swing and hadn't been playing golf at all.

That was the week of the Doral tournament, and I suddenly decided I was going to play golf, to be creative, and that above all else I was going to have fun, have a good time no matter what the results were.

Sure, there were times during the first three rounds at Doral that I had to remind myself to have fun. I had to force it a little, especially when I missed a shot or a putt. But I reminded myself that even the players who win tournaments miss shots. And no matter what had happened on the hole, I walked off each green with a smile on my face. And I did have fun. I shot 68, 69 and 70 and was in sixth place, two strokes back of the leaders, going into the last round.

On Sunday I didn't have to force the fun at all. I shot 65 to win the tournament by two over Jack Nicklaus. That was a lot of fun.

Without doing anything physically different with my game, I had improved 61 places in a week.

That may have been the first time I realized that I played better when I had a good time. I'd always thought it was the other way around. Since then I've always tried to have fun on the golf course first, and I've been pretty successful at it.

Actually, Doc's advice was the much the same as Dave Stockton had given me years before. Dave has one of the best attitudes of anybody who has ever played the game. He is very patient with himself. He has fun, he enjoys the game, he gets excited about it, and he encourages people around him to have fun.

> I realized that I played better when I had a good time.

Being patient and having fun is the key to giving yourself the best opportunity to play well.

He jumped on me one time when I was playing a round with him during my first or second year on Tour. I made a long putt and I didn't smile. He said, "What's the deal? Didn't you enjoy making that 20-footer?" I said I did. He said, "Well, show some enjoyment. Smile a little bit."

For awhile I had to force it. It was uncomfortable, just as a swing change is uncomfortable when you first make it. I felt like I was faking it, like you say "cheese" for the photographer. I'd make a putt and suddenly realize I needed to smile, so I'd put this dinky little smile on my face. But it felt less faked the more I did it, and eventually it became a natural reaction. I may not have the most expressive personality in the world or the prettiest smile, but it's the only one I have, and people now know that I'm smiling. I'll make a putt, tip my hat, say thank you and smile. I'll walk over and talk to Mike Carrick, my caddie, and smile about the putt. Even when the shot is bad, I'll try to force the smile, because that helps on the next shot. People see me having a good time out there, and now it's not faked. It's natural. It's Tom Kite.

But that wasn't me at first, and I guess at times I'll revert. I suppose I had during that period in 1984. But Rotella got me smiling again.

My play has improved accordingly. Doc hit it on the head when he asked me, "When was the last time you were impatient when you were having a good time?"

Being patient and having fun is the key to giving yourself the best opportunity to play well. It doesn't guarantee you'll win, or even play well, but being impatient and having no fun pretty much guarantees that you won't.

One year at Harbour Town I had hit a shot just over the green, about six feet off the putting surface. I took out my 8-iron to make the chip shot, and I chunked it. Just stuck my pick in the ground. The ball moved about three feet.

I was in shock. I looked up at my caddie and he looked at me, and things were pretty tense. Then he said, "Well, it looks like the same club to me."

That broke me up. Then I chipped in for par.

Golf should never be a tragedy. It's fun.

During Saturday's fourth round at the Bob Hope tournament in 1990 one of my pro-am partners was Tommy Smothers, the comedian whose trademark is a yo-yo routine. We had a holdup on the 11th tee and Tommy was entertaining the crowd with his tricks. I made some wise remark, and suddenly Tommy had a brand-new yo-yo in my hands. After I hit my tee shot, I put the yo-yo on my finger and did a few loops and spins (I do have *some* hand-eye coordination) and the crowd cheered. After the amateurs had driven from their tee, we all moved on. Pretty soon the crowd started giggling. There were Tommy and I, 50 yards behind the others, matching yo-yo tricks in the middle of the fairway.

I hadn't exactly given up on my round. I went on to birdie that hole and tie for the tournament lead at that point. But this is not rocket science we're doing. Even though I make my living at golf, it's still just a game.

So have some fun. All kinds of good things are likely to happen.

At any level, other than rank beginner, you can improve your golf game faster by improving your mental processes than by improving your physical skills. Having fun is one of the ways to better manage your mind. Here are some others.

Be what you want to be. There are a lot of bad things that can happen to you on a golf course, and sooner or later they usually do. It is truly a game of misses, and the misses potentially can have a very negative effect on your thinking. But they also are potentially positive, if you make it that way.

It's easy to have a great attitude when everything is going right. It's hard as hell to have the same attitude when things are going wrong. When Tom Watson won the 1982 U.S. Open at Pebble Beach, everybody remembers that he chipped in from the rough on the 17th hole and that's what won him the championship. I think what really won the Open for Tom was the fact that he missed a short putt on the

This is not rocket science we're doing. It's still just a game.

seventh hole and promptly forgot about it. He is one of the best putters who ever played, and he was putting well that year in the Open. Then he missed a short putt in a tournament that meant as much to him as any he had ever played. But he took that miss for nothing more than what it was, an accident, and it didn't faze him. He went on to make a number of putts, including a long one from the fringe on 14, which he is not likely to have done if he had still been worried about missing the short one. Then he hit his tee shot into what looked like an impossible situation on the 17th, one likely to cost him the championship. He told Bruce Edwards, his caddie, that he was going to hole it . . . and he did. That's effective thinking.

Chip Beck has as good an outlook as anybody on Tour today. He's known on Tour as "Gotta love it." It's almost a joke, except that it's very effective for him. If he hits a drive into the trees, he's "gotta love it," because it gives him a great opportunity to recover. If he hits a bad iron shot, he's "gotta love it," because it gives him a chance to scramble. If he hits a shot close to the pin, he's "gotta love it," because it gives him a chance to make a birdie. He has the uncanny ability to look on everything, at least outwardly, as a positive. I suspect that's a learned attitude, that at one point he may have had to fake it. But now it's not fake. It's Chip. And it's fun to watch.

When I lost to Jack Nicklaus by a stroke in the 1986 Masters by missing a ten-footer on the last hole, everybody kept talking about how bad I should feel because I didn't win. I kept stressing it was a good week, that I had played well. I had to do that. For me to play well the next week and the weeks after that, I had to keep thinking about all the good things that happened at Augusta, not that Nicklaus beat me.

In the 1989 U.S. Open at Oak Hill, I had a three-stroke lead standing on the fifth tee the final day. There I hit my tee shot into the water on the right, made triple-bogey and went on to shoot 78. I lost by five strokes. It was a huge disap-

For me to play well the next week, I had to keep thinking about all the good things that happened.

pointment to blow the Open, but if I were going to perform well later I had to take the attitude that I simply didn't win the golf tournament—nothing more, nothing less.

I'll never forget it. I don't forget many of my golf tournaments. But by the next day I'd already started to make it a positive experience. Up to that time I'd not had a particularly good U.S. Open record, so even though I didn't get what I wanted, the trophy, I had played well and had a good finish. I had a wonderful chance to win, and there's no reason to think I won't have a wonderful chance to win future Opens. Maybe the next time I miss a shot like that—and we all miss them—there won't be water there. It will just miss the fairway and I'll be able to knock it up for par or birdie.

I only point out these losses to illustrate that no matter how good a career is—in golf, business or life itself—there are going to be major setbacks. But if you're going to continue to succeed, you have to feed off the positives. I have no choice, nor do you in your game. If you want to play your best golf, you must think in an effective way that produces the desired results. Seeing the negative side of whatever happens is not effective thinking.

Gary Player is one of the most positive persons you could ever imagine. Almost every time he plays somewhere he says, "This is the finest course of its kind I've ever seen." It's a joke among the players and others close to golf. But I don't think it's a joke to Gary. Maybe he's saying it for the members, and it doesn't hurt for them to think they have a great course. Maybe he's saying it for the benefit of the press, so they'll have something to quote him on. But I have a sneaking suspicion that he's saying it for the benefit of Gary Player. He's trying to convince himself that he loves the place and that it's a perfect golf course for him.

I remember calling home after I first saw Waverley Country Club in Portland, site of the 1970 Amateur, and telling my folks that it was made for Lanny Wadkins and me because it was so narrow. And we finished one-two. Gary Player does that every week.

> **If you're going to continue to succeed, you have to feed off the positives.**

A WIN AND A LOSS

The victory interview at Doral in 1984, with runner-up Jack Nicklaus and Steve Melnyk of CBS, was sweet . . . the missed putt on the 72nd hole of the 1986 Masters, which let Nicklaus win, was agonizing.

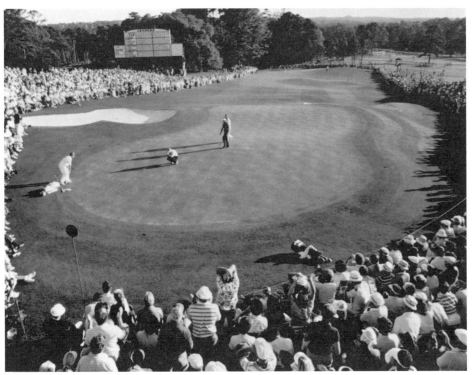

During one of the group discussions we have periodically with Bob Rotella, we were talking about warmup sessions. And Doc said, "If you have a real good warmup session, tell yourself that means you're going to play a good round, because the warmup is so important to how you play that day. If you have a poor warmup session, tell yourself that's great, because every time you hit it poorly on the practice tee it means you're going to play well and the warmup has no relevance to how you will do on the course."

Roger Maltbie said, "Wait a minute, you can't have it both ways. It doesn't make sense to have your warmup session mean something one day and not mean anything the next day. It's not logical."

And Doc replied, "It makes as much sense to do it that way as to do it the other way, *if* what you're trying to do is play well."

He was right, of course. You have to take the attitude that wherever you are at any particular time, that's exactly where you want to be. Because that's your only choice. This is where you are at that moment and you have to go play with it.

You are what you tell yourself you are. You can let doubt creep in, which is negative. Or you can trust what you have, which is positive.

In the 1986 Masters I had trust, and I did everything a man can do to win a golf tournament. I shot 68 the last day. I made an eagle on the eighth hole and was three under on the back nine. I hit a wonderful drive on 18 and a great 6-iron into the green, one of the best iron shots I've ever hit. I hit a wonderful putt. It was as good a routine, as good a tempo, as good a stroke as I've ever made. I totally trusted it. And the putt didn't go in, and I lost the Masters by a stroke. There are no guarantees. But I promise you that I came a lot closer to winning that Masters than I would have if I hadn't trusted.

If you have the capability of shooting 75, and if you have trust in yourself, there is no guarantee that you'll shoot 75 on any given day. But that trust gives you a much better chance.

You are what you tell yourself you are.

Don't let your expectations exceed your limitations. If you're not capable of running a four-minute mile, it's pretty hard to trust that you're going to do that. If you're a 15-handicapper, it's hard to trust that you're going to win the state amateur championship.

Total trust will only allow you to play the best you can at your particular level, at this particular time. But it *will* allow you to do that.

Psychologists tell us that the mind can't tell the difference between positives and negatives, between "do" and "do not." When you stand over the ball and say, "Don't hit this out-of-bounds," as we all have done at times, you might as well be simply saying "out-of-bounds." Because you're thinking about out-of-bounds.

I'll never forget the time Dad and I played in the first National Father-Son Tournament at the Country Club of North Carolina. We were playing a little dogleg par-4 hole with a big lake to the left of the green. Dad was standing over his second shot and he said, "I sure don't want to hit this in the water." I didn't even have a chance to say, "Whoa, back off." Sure enough, he hit the ball in the water. Fortunately, I made my par.

If you tell yourself to hit the ball at the pin, you could also tell yourself *not* to hit the ball at the pin. It doesn't make any difference to the mind. So if you want to hit the ball in the fairway, look at the fairway and think fairway. If you want to hit the ball on the green, think green. If you want to hit the ball in the bunker, think about not hitting the ball in the bunker. More times than not, according to the psychologists, it's going to end up in the bunker.

The mind can't tell the difference between positives and negatives.

Best you just think about hitting it at the target and not worry about the trouble lurking elsewhere. Yes, I know I told you in the last chapter to play away from trouble and now I'm telling you to ignore it. Well, you have to play intelligently. Plan the shot carefully, taking into account the conditions and the hazards. But once you're over the ball and are ready to hit the shot, focus on the target and not all the bad places.

The single most important factor in the game, if you can play just a little bit, is having confidence in your ability to do what you are capable of doing. That's true whether you're playing golf, giving a speech, running a business or participating in any other activity.

There's a lot that goes into that. The ability to recognize your assets and your limitations, the ability to be patient and the discipline to get it done all feed into the making of a confident person. Without confidence, without trust, you're not going to play as well as you're capable of playing.

Get into the zone. I'm not sure there has ever been a good definition of concentration or how to achieve it. The ultimate in concentration is when we get into a "zone," when our thinking is clear, we're focused on the task at hand and we let nothing interfere with that.

You do that by practicing your concentration, by disciplining yourself to pay attention. Discipline is really the key to concentration. You have to discipline yourself on the golf course the same way you do on your job or anything else you do.

Discipline and concentration also are a matter of being interested. When I was a student at Texas, there were certain subjects I loved, and I could get totally immersed in those subjects. The television in my room could be blasting, or the radio could be on, or my roommate could be talking with a friend, and I could be sitting there studying and never miss a beat. I was totally involved.

That's the way you have to be in golf. You have to be totally immersed in what you're doing. You have to be excited about it. It has to mean something to you. If it does, you'll concentrate on it. You won't be distracted. You'll be in a zone.

Jack Nicklaus once missed a short putt on one of the late holes in the Canadian Open, and it cost him the tournament. He said later in a television interview that his shadow was

Discipline and concentration are a matter of being interested.

You can always find a distraction if you're looking for one.

over the hole and that distracted him.

I had never in my life thought about a shadow being over the hole until Jack brought it up. So I had to see if I were missing something. The next day I went to the practice green and hit putts with my shadow in various positions over the hole. I practiced those putts until my shadow didn't bother me. So now when I have to make a putt with my shadow over the hole, it doesn't bother me. I've already tested it, so I never think about it.

This is not a knock at Jack Nicklaus, whose powers of concentration have been better than almost anybody who has every played the the game. It just shows that even the best sometimes let it slip a little.

You can always find a distraction if you're looking for one—the galleries, the roar of the crowd, the guy flipping hamburgers or the birds singing in the trees. That's just as true for you as it is for us on Tour. There's always an available excuse—somebody moved, somebody made a noise, your grip slipped. When you get right down to it, all it means is that you missed the shot. And sooner or later you're going to have to account for that missed shot. So you'd better get involved and excited so you can concentrate on the task at hand and not let all that silly stuff bother you.

For me, getting into a zone usually means I'm thinking tempo and routine and I'm in a totally trusting mindset. If you're analyzing every shot for mechanical flaws, sooner or later you're going to find some and it's going to be very difficult for you to trust.

Much has been said about pressure, tension level and choking in competition. Well, feeling pressure is great. That means you're excited. It means your concentration is high, your adrenaline is pumping. When you're excited about something, your tension level naturally is going to increase.

It's when you can't handle it well that you choke. Choking is basically a loss of concentration. You get out of the present tense. You start thinking about the consequences instead of the act. You lose concentration when you shouldn't. Everybody loses concentration when something is not important to them. If your mind wanders when you're reading a bad novel, it's not because you're choking. It's because you're bored. Choking is letting your mind wander when you should be concentrating on something that you want to do well.

When you do that, you get out of the zone, and you usually forfeit your chances of doing well.

Control your emotions. When I was a little kid, I was playing with Dad one afternoon, and I got mad. I missed a putt and took a divot out of the green. Dad told me to go in and tell Mr. Penick what I had done. I didn't want to, but he told me we weren't leaving the club until I told him, so finally I did.

I think it was the worst thing I've ever had to do. And Mr. Penick understood. He just told me that it was all right, but don't do it again. He knew the punishment already had been handed down, that he didn't need to add anything else.

I've never forgotten the incident. It doesn't keep me from getting angry on the course today, but it does keep me from damaging the golf course or my clubs or other players.

Actually, I think getting angry is part of playing well. I think you have to be a little feisty. You have to hate missing shots. If you don't, then you're going to miss a lot of shots. But you can't let that anger get out of control to the point that you're tearing up greens or affecting other players' games.

Nor can you let it affect your game. Get upset, sure, but get the anger under control before you start to plan your next shot. A little bit of anger means you care and are going to play harder, to pay more attention. Uncontrolled anger means you're going to ruin your round.

You also have to control your fear. It wasn't until I started working with Doc and we began having group meetings that I realized everybody goes through the same thing I was going through in the heat of competition. Everybody has fear. It's a subject that's not talked about on Tour. Nobody wants to admit it, because they think that might give the competition

You have to hate missing shots. If you don't, then you're going to miss a lot of shots.

273

Fear comes in two packages—fear of failure and, sometimes, fear of winning.

an edge. Except that the competition is going through the same thing.

No matter how calm somebody looks out there, he's nervous. Maybe he's scared to death. Maybe he's about to throw up. He wonders whether he can function. That's true for Jack Nicklaus all the way down to the guy trying to win his first golf tournament, or the rawest rookie teeing off in his first event. Or for the guy trying to win the fifth flight in his club championship, or make a three-foot putt on the 18th green to win his nassau bet.

As I said earlier, if you hit the ball well on the practice tee but not as well on the course, it's because it doesn't mean anything on the practice tee and it means a lot to you on the course. Fear comes in two packages—fear of failure and, sometimes, fear of winning.

You overcome fear by reverting to the attitude that works best for you rather than dwelling on the consequences of the shot. If you have a "don't-give-a-damn" attitude on the practice tee and it works well there, then take that attitude to the golf course. Whenever you're worried about the results of a shot, whether it will affect your winning or losing, remember that there are 700 million or so people in China who couldn't care less. It's not that big a deal.

Of course, *you* care, and you should care, but only to the extent that you make the best swing possible without worrying about the consequences. Everybody who has ever played the game has hit good shots and has missed shots. Everybody who has subjected himself to competition has tried and failed. It's disappointing, but it's not a matter of life or death.

You have to turn fear into a positive. Any situation that is important to you, that excites you, gets the adrenaline pumping. The butterflies start flying in your stomach, your hands start sweating and you get a lump in your throat. But adrenaline can be a tremendous asset if you use it correctly. Adrenaline enables you to do superhuman things. It provokes you to run faster than you ever have before. It enables you to lift a car if your child is trapped underneath. Or, on a less critical level, it helps you hit a golf ball farther than you know how. Your adrenaline is always going to flow in times of excitement or stress. If you face a critical situation and the adrenaline isn't working, it means you don't care about what's happening or you're dead.

But you have to know how to control it to make it work *for* you rather than *against* you. You're going to tend to swing faster when you're excited. I'm sure you've noticed that. But amateurs don't have a monopoly on that. We all have that tendency. And if you swing too fast, you're not going to make solid contact and you'll lose distance rather than gain it.

I have to face the adrenaline, the fear, almost every day I play golf, certainly late in every tournament and especially if I have a chance of winning. I control it by thinking of *tempo and routine,* and I suggest that you do too. Anticipate that you're going to swing faster and concentrate on swinging slowly. If you try to swing ultra-slow, you'll probably swing at about your normal speed. You'll hit the ball solidly and probably a little farther because of the adrenaline, so take that into account.

Play from your creative brain. Early in my career I did not give myself a chance to win as often as I might have because I was not in the trusting mindset. I did not, when I was coming down the stretch in a tournament, go to tempo and routine, to the creative side of my brain. I loved to practice and I loved to be analytical, so I tended to have mechanical thoughts. The problem was that that allowed me to practice very well but didn't necessarily allow me to play well when I had to. When I had a problem on the course, I almost always worked on my swing instead of playing golf.

Through trial and error and talking to a lot of people, especially Doc Rotella, I became more and more aware that I played better under pressure, when I needed to play well, when I became very creative and less analytical.

If the adrenaline isn't working, it means you don't care about what's happening or you're dead.

275

Moving from
the analytical
side of the
brain to the
creative side
has helped me
hit the shots
I want.

Tempo and routine were the crutches that allowed me to do this, and they still are. They allow me to hit a little cut shot, a draw, a high or a low shot, the shot I want to hit. I was always able to make a swing that would produce the shot I wanted, but because I was in a mechanical frame of mind I wasn't always able to do it under pressure. I might make a good mechanical swing, but the ball didn't go where I wanted it to.

Ridding myself of mechanical thoughts, moving from the analytical left side of the brain to the creative right side has helped me hit the shots I want when I need them.

Psychologists say that you play your best when your mind is a void, when you just get up and react and hit it. That may be the ideal, but I've never been able to do that. It's difficult for me to keep my mind totally inactive. So I try to keep it filled with thoughts of tempo and routine.

Sometimes the swing thoughts do creep in. One of the best drives I ever hit, under the circumstances, was at the 18th hole in the final round of the 1989 Players Championship. I's a long par 4 with water all the way down the left. I had a two-shot lead over Chip Beck, and the last thing I wanted to do was hit the ball left. I focused on a dead tree through the fairway as my target and thought about tempo, but I also was thinking of clearing my hips to make sure the ball didn't go left. The more I clear the hips, the less tendency I have to hit the ball in that direction.

The result was a dynamite drive that put me in position to make par and win the tournament.

So you can and will have swing thoughts, especially while you're learning to trust your swing. But keep them to a minimum. Two swing thoughts are too many. One may be okay. Zero is best. And if you have to have a swing thought, keep it the same throughout the round. Don't jump from thought to thought. If your swing thought works for the first two holes and doesn't work on the third, you probably just made a bad swing. If you change your thought every time you hit a bad shot, your game will be in shambles.

IT WAS A VERY GOOD YEAR

The Players Championship (above) early in 1989 was the best victory . . . the Nabisco Championships at the end of the year was the richest.

You can have the best swing thought in the world and a great feeling for your swing and still make a bad swing. That's because you have a pulse. You're human. Nobody is perfect. But don't abandon what you're doing because you make a human mistake.

Swing thoughts, swing keys, can change every week or every day. That's not ideal, but they will. But work on them on the practice tee as much as you can and carry them to the course as little as possible.

> The goal is that you should be into playing, not into mechanics.

The goal is that, however you choose to implement it, you should be into playing, not into mechanics. Train on the practice tee to improve your mechanics. Train on the practice tee to learn how to play by playing games. But when you get to the golf course, don't train. Just play. Be creative and let it go. That's what the best players do when they play their best.

Use your imagination. Playing with imagination is part of playing creatively. I discussed in Chapter 2 the need to visualize your shots. Well, you have to imagine it before you can visualize it. This is particularly true with a trouble shot, an out-of-the-ordinary shot, but it comes into play on all shots. It's easier to do when you're standing on a tee with the ball on a peg and looking at a fairly wide-open hole. But you still have to imagine the ball going into the fairway with a little draw or a little fade, whatever shot you are trying to play.

Imagination gives you the ability to handle a situation that you've never encountered before. You might have faced something similar, but never this exact shot. So you have to use your imagination, which is really nothing more than feeding off past experiences.

It's impossible to imagine or visualize something you've never done or can't do. If you took somebody who had never played golf and told him to imagine hitting a high cut around a tree or imagine drawing a ball around a dogleg, he wouldn't have a clue as to what you were talking about. He's never done it. If you're a chronic slicer who has never hit a right-to-left shot in your left, there's no way you're going to be able to imagine drawing a ball around that dogleg.

The thing that makes the trouble shots we play on Tour look so great to the folks in the gallery watching us is that they've never done that. So they can't imagine doing it. We've done it, usually a lot of times. Therefore it's easier for us to imagine the shot, and we can pull it off. We are feeding off prior experiences.

Part of the answer for most players is mechanical. Learn to hit the different shots. The other part requires that you pay attention. When you face a situation, when you hit a certain kind of shot, put that in your computer, as I've said. Enter it in your data bank. Then you'll be able to draw on that experience when you face a similar situation, and you may be able to imagine yourself down the fairway or out of the trees.

Practice your patience. Even today, my biggest problem is being patient on the golf course. Even when I'm playing well, I tend to get impatient. In fact, that's when I tend to become *most* impatient. I seem to have the most patience when I'm not playing well. I'm more tolerant with myself, because I don't have the expectations I do when I'm playing well. When I'm playing well, however, I'm harder on myself. I start pressing to win, and often I get in my own way. I guess I don't really play stupidly, but I start forcing shots, trying to make things happen. I lose my patience, and usually the things that happen are not good.

In the 1990 Bob Hope tournament I was near the lead in the fourth round. I had just made a marvelous recovery shot on the 17th hole and then missed a short putt. The 18th at the Palmer Course, where we were playing, is a par 5 that you can reach in two if you want to risk a carry over water. After my drive I had 229 yards to the pin, 215 to carry over the water, but I had a downhill lie. Mike didn't like the chances, but I wanted to get that bogey back. I had to hit a 4-wood because of the lie, and even though it looked pretty good, I mis-hit it slightly and it fell short into the water. On a lot of

When I'm playing well, I start pressing to win, and often I get in my own way.

other holes it would have bounced onto the green and I'd have had a two-putt for birdie. But balls don't bounce much out of water. So I made a bogey 6 instead of a birdie 4 . . . and lost the tournament by two strokes.

I was impatient, and it cost me.

That's why we play four-day golf tournaments instead of just one day. I don't often lead golf tournaments after the second or third round. But I keep myself in position, and often by the fourth day I have a chance to win. That's why you have to realize that a round of golf is 18 holes, not one or two. If you make a double-bogey on the first hole, there still is plenty of time to make it up . . . if you're patient.

I'm better than I used to be, but I'm still not as patient as I need to be. Some people are naturally patient, I guess, but for most of us patience is a learned behavior. You develop patience just as you learn to smile at those missed shots. At first you fake it. You just have to tell yourself that nothing's going to bother you, and if something does you have to dismiss it as quickly as possible. And you have to do that every time you play golf, until it become second nature.

Don't try to win. It sounds funny, I know, to say that you shouldn't try to win a golf tournament, or a match, or a bet with your pals, because that's what we're all trying to do. That's the fun of it. But there's a fine line between trying hard and trying too hard. I go right back to patience. You can't force something over which you have no control.

And, in the end, you don't have any control over winning or losing. I never have a clue as to when I'm going to win. You have control over how well you play. You don't really have any control over what happens to a shot. You don't have control over what score you ultimately shoot. The only thing you have control over is your attitude and how well you swing.

You're seldom going to make a perfect swing, because that's a difficult thing to do. You're never going to play a perfect round, because there is no such thing. What you can

> You have to realize that a round of golf is 18 holes, not one or two.

do is have as good an attitude as possible and make your swing as good as possible. The better job you do of that, the better job you're going to do coming down the final holes of a tournament, and that usually will translate into some very good scores. Those good scores may even produce a victory.

There are so many different ways of winning and losing golf tournaments that nothing surprises me any more. I've played great and won golf tournaments, and I've played great and lost. I've played poorly and lost. And I've played awful and won.

As I said earlier, I did everything I could have done, and everything I should have had to do, to win the 1986 Masters. And Jack Nicklaus, who was not even in contention for most of the tournament, shot seven under par over the last 10 holes to beat me by a stroke. I had no control over something like that.

At Bay Hill in 1989, Davis Love III and I came to the 72nd hole tied for the lead. I hit my second shot in the water and made double-bogey. Then Davis hit his second shot over the green, stubbed a pitch shot and also made double-bogey. Then I beat him in the playoff. The regulation finish was a comedy of errors. Still, we both had played well for 71 holes. Nobody else had the opportunity to double-bogey the last hole and still get into a playoff. That's why we have 72-hole tournaments.

Even in match play, which is what most amateurs do, you have no control over your opponent. Bobby Jones always used to say he played the course, not his opponent, in match play, and that's a pretty good idea. No matter what the situation looks like, it can change in a moment. Your opponent can hit it in the water and you can hit it in the hole . . . or vice-versa.

So be patient. Don't force it. Do the best you can, whether it's playing the back nine on Sunday at Augusta three under par or making double-bogey on the last hole. Things will sort themselves out and you'll win or you'll lose. That's the only way you can approach it.

Have as good an attitude as possible and make your swing as good as possible.

Worry of any kind is the worse thing you can take onto the golf course.

Have an uncluttered mind. I married Christy Brandt in 1975, and that may have been the best thing that ever happened to my career and my life. She has been the support I've leaned on over the years. She has seen me through the bad times and the good. She has helped me when I've been down, and she has been patient when I've been up, when there are so many demands on my time.

From a physical and logistical standpoint, she handles all my travel arrangements and most of the bookwork. That leaves my mind uncluttered to concentrate on golf.

Christy is the No. 1 wife on Tour. Admittedly, that's a biased viewpoint, but you could find others who would agree. And, if you look at the successful players, you'll see that most of them have that kind of support.

The point here is not that your spouse should support your golf activities, unless you make your living at it. But there certainly should be no objection, because then you're going to worry about that. And worry of any kind is the worse thing you can take onto the golf course. If you're having marital trouble, if you have a problem at the office, if you're worried about your kids in college or your next business trip, and if you take that onto the course, you're not going to play well.

Leave your troubles behind at the first tee. You'll play better and have more fun, and that's why you're out there.

Winning feeds on winning. My first couple of victories in the '70s didn't have much influence on my confidence or my career, because they took so long and were so far apart. It wasn't until 1981 that the wins started feeding off of one another. It was a gradual thing, but when you start winning every year, it's a great confidence booster to realize that you're one of the top players and that top players win golf tournaments. That's true at my level and it's true at yours.

After winning at least one tournament for seven consecutive years prior to 1988, I went almost a year and a half without a victory. In 1988 I had three second-place finishes, including a playoff loss to Curtis Strange in the Nabisco

Championships, and finished fifth on the money list with $760,405. But I didn't win, and I suppose there were critics who were thinking I was too old to win again.

I hope I laid that myth to rest in 1989. I won at Bay Hill in early March and at The Players Championship the next week. Then I won the season-ending Nabisco Championships in a playoff over Payne Stewart. That earned me PGA Player of the Year honors and the money title with a record $1,395,278, and it made me the first player in history to go over $5 million in earnings. In 1990, with my victory at Memphis, that became $6 million.

The victories in 1989 were nice, particularly because they came on quality courses against quality fields. The Players Championship may not yet be a major, whatever that means, but it will be some day. Tradition takes a little time. It's certainly the best tournament I've ever won.

The money is not that important. It does not make me better than Jack Nicklaus or any of the other great players. With the escalation in purses, someone will surely pass me some day. The fact that, for the moment, I'm the all-time leading money winner means only that I've been a consistently good player for a long time.

As far as I'm concerned, the more significant statistic is that I was No. 1 in scoring for the decade of the '80s with an average of 70.57 for every round played on the PGA Tour. As I said at the start of this book, that's what golf is all about.

It is so much more fun to play golf well than it is to play it poorly.

I have not done all I want to do in golf. Like anything else, golf is a learning process, and I have a lot more to learn.

We all have dreams. Anybody who plays the game with any seriousness at all wants to become a better player. I do and you do, and my dream is no more important to me than yours is to you. No matter what your level of talent or dedication, it is so much more fun to play golf well than it is to play it poorly. And the fun of it is why we all try to improve, why we all dream.

I hope this book will help fulfill some of those dreams.

AFTERWORD

The one guy you can't beat is the guy who just keeps coming.

In an earlier, different incarnation, when I was working in Boston and New York, I used to cover a lot of boxing. That's more or less at the other end of the sports spectrum from golf . . . considerably lower on the food chain, I suppose you could say.

But it was fun, back there in the late '50s and early '60s. Lots of characters in the fight business back then. More hangers-on than in any other sport. Unless it might be golf. But that's a different story.

There were a large number of very good middleweights and welters in those days. People even paid attention to them. So did television. Joey Giardello, Terry Downes, Gene Fullmer, Dick Tiger, Paul Pender, Kid Paret and the man who killed him, Emile Griffith. Tony DeMarco and Carmen Basilio. Some good middles who never won a title but were big TV attractions, Tiger Jones and, out on the West Coast, Art Aragon. And, of course, the real Sugar Ray, the best of them all.

The old Madison Square Garden was in operation on

Eighth Avenue back then. On Friday nights in the dark and grungy bars—most of them with Irish names—around the Garden, the trainers and seconds, the sparring partners and the beat-up old fighters with their broken noses and broken shoes would gather to cadge drinks and tell stories and pass judgment on the fighters on the screen.

Often their attention span was very short. Sometimes they'd lapse into mumbles and, shuffling and stumbling, re-live fights from other times and other places. Memories were clouded, uncertain and faulty. They'd argue about who did what to whom. They'd fuss and fret, fumble and mumble because no one remembered it the way they did, and no one could agree.

But they always agreed on one thing. You can beat a dancer, they'd say. And you can beat a hitter. But the one guy you can't beat is the guy who just keeps coming. You can hit him and hurt him, you can cut him and knock him down, but if he just keeps coming, you're not going to beat him. That was the guy they admired.

Had they known anything about golf—those broken-down, punchy old fighters with the scarred eyes and lumpy ears—they'd have liked Tom Kite. They'd have admired him.

He's a guy who just keeps coming.

He's been hit and hurt. The cuts and scars are not visible, but they're there. He's been knocked down and on the ropes.

But he just keeps coming.

You're not going to beat him. Not in the long run.

He keeps coming at you.

He is the ultimate grinder. You may slow him. You may hurt him. But he just keeps coming, just keeps grinding away.

I've seen it so many times in so many places.

There's the memory of the time, in 1978, when he called that penalty on himself at Pinehurst. He'd only won one tournament at the time. He was still in the process of estab-

> You're not going to beat him. Not in the long run.

lishing himself. And he was in the hunt for another title. But as he stood over a putt, in the address position, the ball moved. A tiny fraction of an inch. No one else saw it, not his fellow players nor the caddies. But Tom saw it. He called a penalty on himself. And it cost him the tournament. He lost by one stroke. And he was furious. Because he hadn't played one stroke better. Not because of the penalty. He seemed astounded that anyone would mention the penalty. It didn't occur to him to do anything else. It's the way the game is played. So he lost the tournament.

But he kept on coming. He won the B.C. Open the following week.

He's had more than his share of disappointments. There was the time in '82, at the Bob Hope Classic, when he was victimized by Ed Fiori's 80-foot birdie putt in a playoff. But Kite kept grinding, kept on coming. He won at Bay Hill a couple of months later.

He has won with frequency and consistency. Twice he has been named the Golf Writers Association Player of the Year. He's won the Vardon Trophy for the best scoring average, and led the money winners. At this writing, in fact, he's the game's all-time leader at the pay window. He's an accomplished, respected player.

But his best moments have been in his triumphs over adversity, in his ability to turn a negative into a positive.

He led the final round of the '84 Masters until a 7-iron shot spun back off the bank and into the water on the 12th hole.

A day later, at Hilton Head Island, S.C., he said it was all very encouraging, that he'd proved to himself he had the game to win in the majors.

He kept on coming and won two tournaments that year.

He's had other near misses in the majors—a runner-up spot in the '78 British Open and the '83 and '86 Masters, the latter when a 72nd-hole birdie putt failed to fall. And he had a back-nine lead in the '86 British Open until a tee shot ended up in an impossible position and he made triple bogey.

It hurt. But he kept on coming.

His best moments have been in his triumphs over adversity.

The '89 season could serve as a summary of his career. It included achievement and disappointment, big losses, big victories.

To get the full flavor, you have to go back to the end of '88 and the season-ending Nabisco Championships. Kite and Curtis Strange were in the race for Player of the Year and money-winning honors. It all came down to the Nabisco. Kite and Strange tied after the regulation 72 holes. In a day-late playoff, Strange won it—and all the other honors—on the 17th hole at Pebble Beach.

Now go to '89.

Kite scored consecutive victories at Bay Hill and in the Players Championship. He was on top of the world. In the U.S. Open at Oak Hill, he had a last-round lead . . . then saw a tee shot drift to the right into a creek he didn't even know existed. He lost it. He went from the heights to the depths, the pits, as it were.

But Kite, as persistent as crabgrass, just kept on coming, kept on grinding.

He went back to the season-ending Nabisco. It was all on the line again—the money title, Player of the Year, all of that. This time he won it in a playoff. Won Player of the Year. Set a single-season money-winning record. He just kept on coming, kept on grinding 'til he got it.

He is a symbol of all that is good in golf. He has honesty and integrity, perseverance and skill. He adheres to the work ethic. He is a good man. He is my friend.

The old fighters would have loved him.

He won't quit. He just keeps coming at you.

Bob Green
Associated Press

> He is a symbol of all that is good in golf.